GREAT RIDING SCHOOLS
OF THE WORLD

GREAT

RIDING SCHOOLS OF THE WORLD

DORIAN WILLIAMS

Foreword by HRH THE DUKE OF EDINBURGH
President of the Fédération Equestre Internationale

Preface by William Steinkraus
President of the United States Equestrian Team

With photographs by John Hedgecoe

THE MACMILLAN PUBLISHING CO., INC.
New York

Macmillan Publishing Co., Inc.
866 Third Avenue, New York, N.Y. 10022

First American Edition 1975

Library of Congress Cataloging in Publication Data

Williams, Dorian.
  Great riding schools of the world.

  1. Riding schools. I. Title.
SF310.A1W54 1975   798'.23'071   74–14906
ISBN 0–02–629060–X

Printed in Great Britain

CONTENTS

Foreword

by His Royal Highness, Prince Philip, Duke of Edinburgh
President of the Fédération Equestre Internationale

People can teach themselves to do almost anything and many people who have achieved success are proud to say that they are self-taught. The system works but only when there is exceptional talent and then exceptional application. If we relied on that system alone each generation would have to re-discover every lesson learned since Xenophon wrote his treatise on horsemanship. Far better results will always be achieved by a combination of natural talent and good basic instruction. Good instruction in its turn comes from the accumulation and refinement of experience and the rational application of consistently successful techniques.

Riding and driving horses is almost unique among man's activities. It is the only one which requires an intimate and understanding partnership between man and an animal. In most other cases only man has to learn or be taught; in riding and driving both man and the animal need to acquire the special skills and techniques.

This is where riding schools differ from all other training establishments and why they play such a vital part in maintaining proper standards of horsemanship. It is one thing to teach yourself to ride or drive without assistance but it is a very different matter to train a horse by instinct or simply by reading books.

In this splendid book the author has set out with great clarity the particular contributions which some of the more famous riding schools of the world have made to the perpetuation of the highest standards of horsemanship. Mr Dorian Williams, who has already done so much to promote the arts and sports of riding, has now added a volume of quite exceptional interest. I hope it will remind all who read it how much our pleasures as riders and drivers depend on those who learn the lessons of the past and take so much trouble to pass them on to those who wish to learn.

Preface

by William Steinkraus
President of the United States Equestrian Team

The art of riding is both complex and subtle; so much so that I have never known a good horseman of whatever age who did not feel that he was still learning about it. Of course, there are also others whose minds are shuttered tight, either in ignorance, or in narrow dogmatism, which can be even worse. The category of those who do know something but think they know everything is not especially rare, for stubborn fools have graduated from the best riding schools just as they have from Yale and Oxford. In the end, education still depends on the quality of learning rather than the quality of teaching.

For all of this, the best way to learn any difficult and complex subject is to study it systematically, drawing from past knowledge. The axiom that those who will not learn from history are doomed to repeat it is especially true of riding, as anyone who has worked entirely alone can attest. And so it follows that man's progress in the equestrian art depends upon the systematic transmission of accrued knowledge about it.

This transmission has taken place in two principal ways. First, through the written word, starting with Xenophon and proliferating rapidly, after the invention of printing, from Grisone down to the present day. The second way has been through oral instruction and practical demonstration, as customarily offered in the serious kinds of riding academy discussed in this book.

There are admittedly less serious riding academies that could be better described as hack stables, and it is because of these that the word 'academy' in connection with riding has lost some of its elegant connotations in the passage of time. (Hence the title of this book, no doubt.) Nonetheless, the usage has an impeccable lineage, reaching back to the courtly renaissance academies of the sixteenth century that followed the famous establishments of Pignatelli and Fiaschi at Naples.

Like most other things, riding academies have generally reflected the social and economic circumstances of their times. They tended to remain satellites of royal courts until revolutionary pressures drove them to the shelter of the military establishment. There they retained an élite status and, as cavalry schools, continued to serve as the prime repositories of systematic equestrian knowledge until the end of World War II. At that point, the general mechanisation of horse cavalry found ordinary horse lovers faced for the first time with the challenge of assuming the principal burden of supporting them.

The challenge still remains. It is interesting to examine the riding schools described in this book from the viewpoint of their economic support as well as from those of organisation, physical facilities and curricula. Some are old, some relatively new. Some depend entirely on private, civilian support; some benefit partially or primarily from government funding; some few retain a trickle of military funds, though the élite branch of the military has long since taken to the air.

Obtaining the necessary funds to maintain even a small national equestrian centre is a demanding task, as I know from first-hand experience. Yet the kinds of institutions described in the following pages not only constitute a precious part of our heritage from the past, but are perhaps also the key element in the future of world equestrian sport. Thus it is my fervent hope that this handsome and interesting book will, by focusing interest on the various private and national equestrian centres it surveys, expose to a wider public both their enduring value and importance for the future, as well as their present status as an endangered species.

For if equestrian sport as we know and enjoy it is to survive and prosper, so must they.

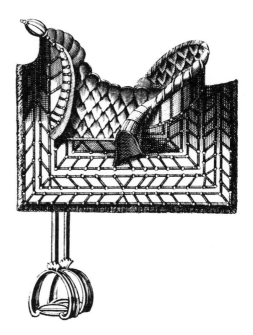

Acknowledgments

First I would like to express my gratitude to His Royal Highness The Duke of Edinburgh, not only for writing a foreword for this book but also for the importance he has attached, as President of the Fédération Equestre Internationale, to a high standard of instruction at international level, as well as to the value of a high standard of international competitive riding. This led directly to the Conference at the National Equestrian Centre, Stoneleigh, for Fédération Equestre Internationale Instructors, which was attended by representatives of most of the riding schools included in this book.

I am indebted too to the great co-operation I have received from the principals, commandants and chief instructors of the schools concerned: from Colonel Hans Handler, Commandant of the Spanish Riding School of Vienna; Lieutenant-Colonel Boisfleury, *écuyer en chef* at Saumur, and Colonel de St André, his predecessor; Bertalan de Nemethy and Jack le Goff, the Team Trainers at Gladstone, New Jersey; Major John Lynch, the Director at Morven Park, Virginia; Hans Ernmark, Secretary-General of both the Swedish Horse Society and the Swedish Equestrian Federation; also Anders Gernandt of Swedish Television; Günther Festerling, Director of the Deutsche Reitschule, Warendorf; also Dr Dietmar Specht, an eminent veterinary surgeon and organiser of the equestrian events in the Munich Olympic Games; Colonel Schummelketel, Editor of *De Hoefslag* and Founder-Director of Deurne, and Jan Bardoel, the present Director of Deurne; Mikhail Sergei Ivanov, Director of the Burevestnik Riding Club, Izmailova, Moscow; Dr Gian Franco Boveri, Principal of the Centro Ippico di Castellazzo, Milan; also Count Enrico Buschetti, President of the Federazione Italiana Sport Equestri; Paul and Monica Weier, proprietors of Elgg; Don Carlos Kirkpatrick O'Donnell, Director of the Club de Campo, and his head of staff Señor Sesinando; and Antonio Alvarez Acedo, Senior Instructor of the Club Deportivo Las Lomas, both of Madrid; also the Duke of Aliaga, a leading member of the former club; Captain Ian Dudgeon, proprietor of Burton Hall, Dublin, and Sylvia Stanier, Chief Instructor: and many others on the staff, at all levels, of these establishments.

In particular, however, I owe a very deep gratitude to Michael Clayton, Editor of *Horse and Hound*, and Charles Stratton, both of whom co-ordinated a very great deal of research in a most helpful and efficient manner, travelling many miles to do so: to Brigadier Dick Hobson, Dawn Dray and Priscilla Phipps whose knowledge and experience of America, France and Russia respectively were of enormous assistance.

Finally my thanks are due to Wendy Russell and Brenda Crook for typing and re-typing the many drafts of the different chapters.

Introduction

I t was in the late sixteenth and early seventeenth centuries that the great riding schools of the world came into vogue. They were attached to the magnificent courts of Europe and to many of the famous aristocratic households where, almost invariably, an eminent riding master was retained.

Xenophon, two thousand years earlier, had written his famous treatise on horsemanship, but with the decline of the Greek and Roman empires, horsemanship had been relegated to a utility exercise, riding being only a means of transport; the horse, therefore, was regarded solely as a beast of burden. It was not until the end of the sixteenth century that riding in Europe was once again regarded as an art; it was even considered a science. With this change of spirit great riding schools came into being. For the most part they were concerned with High School riding, and what is now considered unique to the Spanish Riding School in Vienna was more or less commonplace.

The hey-day of the great riding schools was surprisingly short-lived. The Spanish Riding School, fortunately, is still in existence, and perhaps more active than at any time in its four-hundred-year history. Most of the other schools, however, due to the exigencies of war, became military academies; at the turn of the nineteenth century, the elegance of *haute école* was replaced by a more practical sense of horsemanship and horsemastership. During the twentieth century, with the development of mechanised transport, the once flourishing riding establishments suffered further. As the cavalry regiments in most European countries were disbanded, most of the schools disappeared or at best became appendages to modern military barracks.

After the First World War a new kind of school came into being: this was the commercial riding school run by independent proprietors of the calibre of Colonel Jack Hance and Major Faudel Phillips, who must be regarded as the pioneers in England, and therefore the pioneers of the whole movement, for it was some years before other countries followed suit in providing riding facilities on a commercial basis. It was this break between the disappearance of the old cavalry schools and the appearance of the new commercial schools that was responsible for many of the problems confronting the riding world today; the main problem, of course, being the dearth of good instructors.

In 1971, as a result of discussions at the 1969 meeting of the

PREVIOUS PAGES *A detail from the Alexander Sarcophagus, reflecting the style of riding at the time of Xenophon. Horses were usually ridden bareback, although a padded cloth was used for protection in battle; the bridle is now missing from this detail.*

A battle scene from a twelfth-century manuscript. By this time a saddle with a high cantle and tree had been developed, offering the knight some measure of resistance against being un-horsed by a blow from an adversary's lance.

Fédération Equestre Internationale, a conference of international instructors was convened at the behest of the President, His Royal Highness Prince Philip, Duke of Edinburgh, at the National Equestrian Centre, Stoneleigh, England. Prince Philip himself attended the conference.

Speaking at the opening session, the President of the British Equestrian Federation, Colonel Sir Michael Ansell, said:

'I believe that throughout the world there is almost an explosive growth in the number of persons wishing to ride. It is difficult to assess why this has come about. Perhaps it may be that with shorter working days there is consequently more leisure. Perhaps it may be the desire to take part in some form of "risk" sport.

'I am confident that we all agree that riding and the care of horses and ponies can do nothing but good for the building of character. But any sport or activity of this kind is costly, and the normal person does not like to waste his money and, therefore, in order to get the best out of it one should try to do it *correctly*. Whether it be tennis, golf or riding one must learn the best way to take part, and so get the maximum pleasure. The better one rides, the more fun it is.

'In the pre-war years we were fortunate, as much instruction was provided by officers and non-commissioned officers from "mounted" regiments of the services. However, with the disappearance of the horse from the services, this source of supply has gradually dried up. There can be little doubt that there is now a world shortage of top instructors and the object of this three-day convention is to find how each of us in our various countries gets over this problem – how the many riders are being provided with instruction and how the instructors are trained.'

As Chairman of the conference, I added: 'We hardly expect to find a solution to this problem between now and Thursday evening! On the other hand, neither do we see ourselves as, in the words of our William Shakespeare,

OPPOSITE *Almost without interruption since the seventeenth century, the classical airs of* haute école *have been taught and practised at the Spanish Riding School in Vienna. Painting by J. V. Blaas, 1890.*

RIGHT AND BELOW *Antoine de Pluvinel developed a style of riding that was logical, elegant and refined. As personal riding master to Henry IV of France and later to Louis XIII, he is credited with having introduced* haute école *into France.*

Fig. 16.

LEFT *William Cavendish, Duke of Newcastle, riding instructor to Charles II, painted by Van Dyck. When Charles fled from England Newcastle accompanied him and set up a school in Antwerp where his theories of advanced horsemanship, based on his close study of the mental and physical qualities of the horse, were practised.* ABOVE *The* levade, *an illustration from an eighteenth-century edition of Newcastle's book* New Methods of Dressing the Horse.

silly beggars,
Who sitting in the stocks refuge their shame
That many have and others must sit there;
And in this thought they find a kind of ease
Bearing their own misfortune on the back
Of such as have before endured the like.

In other words, we do not believe that because in other countries (no less than in our own) there is a shortage of instructors, we should just sit back and do nothing about it. Hence this conference, participation in which will, we hope, lead to valuable developments in each of the countries here represented, and far beyond.'

This was the first time that such a conference had been held, or indeed that a full awareness of the problem had been admitted. Most leading countries were represented, including the United States and Russia. Of the major riding nations only Italy was, unfortunately, absent.

The two principal speakers were, appropriately, Colonel Hans Handler, Commandant of the Spanish Riding School of Vienna, and Colonel de St André, at that time *écuyer en chef* of the *Cadre Noir* and Commandant at Saumur. The former, of course, represented the one remaining school in the world where there is complete dedication to one riding art, *haute école*. The latter, interestingly, was able to speak of the gradual transition from the great military academy devoted largely but never entirely to *haute école* at the end of the eighteenth and beginning of the nineteenth centuries, to the predominantly civilian school of today, though, as is recounted in Chapter II of this book, the *Cadre Noir* itself is still retained.

It is obvious that in the world economic climate of today it is virtually impossible for any school to specialise completely in one equestrian discipline: unless, like the Spanish Riding School of Vienna, it has become a major tourist attraction and an indispensable feature of the city, as is the Eiffel Tower of Paris, the Empire State Building of New York and the leaning tower of Pisa.

The nearest equivalent to Vienna, in that it is able to specialise, is the U.S.E.T. Centre at Gladstone, New Jersey, where the United States show jumping teams are trained under Bertalan de Nemethy. But until 1974 even Gladstone was diversified for its facilities

Introduction

were shared with the three-day event riders under Jack le Goff.

The majority of schools are, of necessity, varied in their curricula. Though at many of the major schools there is a concentration on one or other aspect of riding, such as show jumping at Milan and Elgg, the training of instructors at Morven, Virginia, and general equitation at Stoneleigh, few schools can afford not to provide courses and organise instruction on all aspects of riding and even of driving. Some countries are fortunate in that they are subsidised, to a greater or lesser extent, by their respective governments. A few are wholly managed by the government; the majority, however, are dependent upon public support and private enterprise.

The schools covered in this book span a very wide spectrum of the equestrian scene, stretching from the functional efficiency of Strömsholm to the unavoidable opportunism of Stoneleigh, from the splendidly spacious Club de Campo to the traditional austerity of Saumur. One striking feature emerges from this book – the completely contrasting characters of the different riding schools functioning throughout the world. Each has its own personality and its own purpose. Nevertheless, a study of them does seem to show that there is developing, or re-developing, a uniformity in the amenities, if not, as is to be expected, in the style and methods of instruction.

Almost invariably a spacious indoor school is the *sine qua non* of a riding establishment. Sufficient areas in the form of smaller and larger rings or arenas for work on the ground (dressage) are essential; probably more than one jumping arena will be required. More and more there appears to be an awareness of the necessity of a cross-country track, a feature which is obviously expensive and far from easy to construct: plenty of space, good going and a skilled knowledge in constructing cross-country fences are needed. Leading riding nations, almost without exception, now concentrate on three-day eventing as much as on show jumping and dressage.

Today, with the ever-rising costs of labour and forage, stables which are labour-saving in their design are going to be of great advantage. Obviously, therefore, those schools which have only recently come into being, such as Deurne in Holland, are going to gain. On the other hand, some of the older schools are fortunate in that their stables were built when labour and materials were cheap, with the result that a nineteenth-century stable is probably considerably superior to a twentieth-century dwelling house!

Despite this growing uniformity in lay-out, there is no conformity in styles and methods of instruction: probably there never will be. The technique of de Nemethy in the United States could hardly be more different to that of Dick Stilwell in England, but they both achieve results. It is fascinating that although man has been riding horses for over three thousand years, there is still no accepted standard or agreed style. Riding techniques are very much a matter of temperament: hence the discipline of the Germans, the fluency of the French, the animation of the Italians. Fortunately, however, it has long been

OPPOSITE *The Grand Manège at Versailles. Founded by Louis XIV in 1680, the school was closed down during the French Revolution. It was re-established in 1814 under the d'Abzac brothers but dwindled to practically nothing by 1830 without having made any significant contribution.*

Introduction

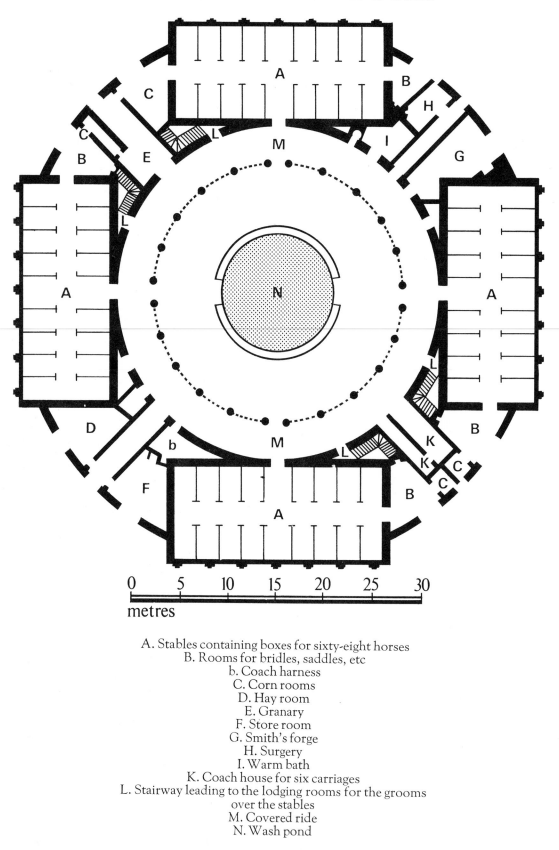

AN EIGHTEENTH-CENTURY PLAN FOR A GENTLEMAN'S STABLE

A. Stables containing boxes for sixty-eight horses
B. Rooms for bridles, saddles, etc
b. Coach harness
C. Corn rooms
D. Hay room
E. Granary
F. Store room
G. Smith's forge
H. Surgery
I. Warm bath
K. Coach house for six carriages
L. Stairway leading to the lodging rooms for the grooms
over the stables
M. Covered ride
N. Wash pond

appreciated that there are certain common factors. At one school the main discipline may be show jumping, on which most of the instruction is concentrated. Show jumping demands accuracy, precision and exactness in timing. At another school the discipline may be three-day eventing, which demands speed, stamina and courage from both horse and rider. But these disciplines demand more than a nodding awareness of the immense value of the third discipline – work on the ground, or dressage as it is now known – whether elementary or advanced. No school can ignore this basic training and the amenities associated with it, for vital in any style of riding is proper balance, the right contact in both hand and leg, and correct weight disposal at the different paces; though in different countries there will be varying and sometimes apparently conflicting emphases.

With an enormous increase in the interest in and popularity of riding, it is of the utmost importance that as many people as possible should be properly taught to ride – even if there are varieties of styles. It is the horse that suffers as a result of bad horsemanship. An awareness of a need for improved instruction the world over is, therefore, of the utmost importance. Gradually there is evidence of a uniformity in the methods employed, which can only have valuable and encouraging results in the context of world equitation. A real improvement can come about only if the leading schools in each country can set an example and, where possible, play a part in producing properly-trained instructors.

The fact that a school has been included in this book does not mean either that it is the only school of importance in its own country, let alone the official national centre, or that there are not many other schools which might well merit inclusion. The title of the book is *Great Riding Schools of the World*, not *The* Great Riding Schools. There can be no doubt that in many countries there are schools not mentioned which are as excellent as the ones chosen. In some countries where riding is particularly popular, as in Britain, Germany and the USA, there are many first-class schools. Obviously they cannot all be included.

A hundred years ago one could have produced a book covering at least twelve establishments of the calibre of the Spanish Riding School of Vienna, Saumur or Tsar Alexis's Izmailova with its fifty thousand horses. Circumstances today have decreed that even the best and most

Introduction

successful riding schools are far more varied and complex, each harshly influenced by commercial necessities.

Nevertheless, each of the schools in this book has achieved much, has aspired to and attained a high standard and has inevitably been a considerable influence on riding, particularly on educated riding and the proper study of equitation in its own country. The exquisite splendour of Vienna is inevitably unique: but who is to say that the cause of equitation is no less served in the strictly practical complex of Warendorf, the modern lay-out of Deurne or the informal efficiency of Burton Hall? Each has a contribution to make. In part this book is a tribute to that contribution. Their influence, some for centuries, some for only a few years, has been and will be of unending benefit to riding and the art of equitation, and to all those who enjoy any or all forms of riding and the arts and sports associated with the horse.

I would like to end this introduction by quoting something written more than fifty years ago by my father, the late Colonel V.D.S.Williams, who, because of the position that he held in so many departments of the horse world in Britain, had an exceptional influence on British equitation after the War.

'It is often assumed that the basic views on training have undergone considerable changes during the past few centuries and that entirely different methods inevitably exist in different countries. This, however, need not be so; nor, I believe, is it. The classical art of riding has varied little during the past one hundred years. In fact the oldest book on equitation in existence, written by Xenophon two thousand years ago, teaches much the same methods of training as are taught today.

'The classical art of riding may be described as the method that aims at obtaining the perfect production of all the *natural* movements of the horse in perfect harmony: perfect harmony between the horse and the rider in a natural way and with full consideration of the psychology of the horse.

'Everything that is contrary to nature, all artificial movements, all artificial methods of obtaining natural movements are outside the classical art of riding. The classical art of riding need not differ according to the country where it is taught, although there are naturally variations due to the temperaments of the different nations.

OPPOSITE *Saumur in the nineteenth century. Under the influence of Pluvinel, pillars were introduced into the training of the* sauteurs *of the* Cadre Noir.

LEFT *François Baucher, a ringmaster at the fashionable Cirque d'Eté, an equestrian circus, was a horseman of rare ability although his methods were unorthodox.* RIGHT *James Fillis, an Englishman and disciple of de Guérinière, became* écuyer en chef *in St Petersburg and an important influence on Russian equitation.*

'The most important schools are [and this was fifty years ago]:

1 The German school at Hanover
2 The French school at Saumur
3 The English school at Weedon
4 The Italian school at Pinerolo
5 The Austrian school at Vienna

The German and French schools are both based on very much the same conception; they aim at producing the highest possible performances with a few selected horsemen in order to set a standard of achievement and to show which methods of training give the best results. They, together with the English school, are based on practical military riding, although on the Continent they contend that in Britain we have no really developed system of training, relying on the excellent character of our horses. There is a saying in Germany that the best trainers in England are the English Thoroughbred stallions. The Italian school on the other hand pays little attention to dressage. It argues that the best method of preparing a horse for cross-country work is by a thorough development of his jumping powers. The Imperial Spanish Riding School is just the reverse; there they cultivate the proper High School riding without paying much attention to its usefulness for cross-country purposes.

'There is, however, one fundamental principle which dates from the time of Xenophon and is common to all schools: that the procedure in training must depend on the end to be attained, the time available, the horse to be trained, and the knowledge, capabilities and temper of the trainer. The measure of achievement in any school is dependent upon the patience, firmness, knowledge and understanding of the instructor. Without these qualities little of value can ever be attained.'

Eadweard Muybridge's photographic experiments in the late nineteenth century enabled men to study the movements of the horse at speed for the first time. This series shows the action of the limbs at the gallop.

The Spanish Riding School
Vienna

OPPOSITE *The great school* quadrille, *the consummate display of horsemanship. Protocol is strictly observed in the riding hall. On entering the riders salute the portrait of Emperor Charles VI, a symbolic gesture of gratitude to the school's first patron.*

Austria

There can be no doubt that when one is talking about the great riding schools of the world pride of place must go to the famous Spanish Riding School of Vienna. Not only is this the oldest school, but it is also the most magnificent.

It was as early as 1572 that the title 'The Spanish Riding Stable' first appeared, from which the present name of the school is derived. It comes from the fact that in the sixteenth century horses of Spanish blood were the most popular for classical riding on account of their strength, intelligence and physical appearance. Today the Spanish School still cultivates High School riding with the famous Lipizzaner stallions – the only remaining descendants of the once proud race of Spanish horses. The opening of the riding school, as we know it today, occurred in September 1735 when fifty-four school stallions, originating from the Royal studs, were first exhibited in the regal surroundings of the present riding hall. Nevertheless, the famous stables had already been in existence in Vienna for some two hundred years.

The magnificent building, familiar to so many today, was begun in 1729. It is a work of the first magnitude and one of the many wonderful creations which emerged from the enthusiasm for building experienced in Vienna after its liberation from centuries of Turkish intimidation. This rare masterpiece of architectural design achieves its crowning glory in the superb, unsupported plaster ceiling, enhanced by the hanging chandeliers reminiscent of the great eighteenth- and nineteenth-century ballrooms in the lavish Courts of Europe. The dimensions of the riding hall, fifty-five by eighteen metres with a height of seventeen metres, are quite exceptional and an even greater impression of depth and grandeur is created by the series of columns and long windows on each side.

Such a riding school is, of course, unique. Its situation on the Josefplatz, adjoining the Hofburg Palace, places it in the very centre of Vienna. The exterior of the building is not particularly impressive, but to the visitor seeing the riding hall for the first time the interior appears to be something almost out of this world. An example of perfect harmony and symmetry, it has remained unaltered for 250 years with its two great galleries bathed in light and resplendent in white and gold. The generous dimensions and structural finesse were realised by the celebrated architect Joseph Emmanuel Fischer von Erlach, one of the great masters of the Baroque period. The execution of the whole building was considered down to the smallest detail, as is evident by the sculptured stone pillars and the careful ornamentation of the ceiling.

Facing the entrance to the riding hall is the emperor's box on the first gallery, inside of which is a portrait of the first patron Charles VI, Emperor of the Holy Roman Empire, on a Lipizzaner stallion. The purpose of the school under his aegis was the preservation of the equestrian art in its most noble form – the High School riding which still characterises the school in Vienna. This painting is the only coloured decoration on the walls of the handsome white hall. In addition, the balustrades of the two balconies surrounding the school are topped with crimson velvet; in the centre of the school – to give another dash of colour – are flags surmounting the two pillars used for the exercises 'above the ground'.

It is almost impossible to enter this great riding hall without being struck with the very awe one feels on entering a cathedral; it has the same atmosphere, the same sense of hush – almost worship. Indeed, the Spanish Riding School has been described more than once as the Temple of the Horse or the Shrine of High School Riding. Nor are these phrases mere exaggerations: to attend one of the performances at the Spanish Riding School in Vienna is an unforgettable experience, whether one is an avid horseman or not. That it should be so splendid is a testimony to the brilliance and popularity of High School riding three and four hundred years ago. In those times equitation in its advanced stages was an art – limited at first to court officials and imperial dignitaries, although later made available to young men of the bourgeoisie and foreign officers. The aim of High School riding, whose popularity spread all over Europe, was to pursue horsemanship to its highest form of perfection. Even in Britain, which at this period was seeing the sudden upsurge of interest in foxhunting as a national sport, the great Duke of Newcastle was trying to encourage people in the art of advanced equitation and, indeed, he was responsible for a manual, *New Methods of Dressing the Horse*, which is still highly respected today wherever dressage is practised.

Few would disagree with the contention that the Spanish Riding School is the greatest attraction Vienna has to offer to the hundreds of thousands of tourists who visit the city each year. Indeed it is becoming increasingly difficult for the ordinary visitor to get hold of a ticket for

OVERLEAF *A performance of the quadrille in the grounds of Schönbrunn Castle on the school's 400th anniversary.*

the famous Sunday afternoon performances in the school. But what an experience these performances are! From the moment of taking one's place there is a tremendous sense of anticipation.

The school is remarkable in yet another respect; it is only Lipizzaner stallions that are used for the work and the displays. The Lipizzaners have a proud past. With their graceful movements, so well suited to the Spanish Riding School, they are successors to the noble Spanish breed of horses whose representatives were never absent at any of the early performances and carousels. Even in the days of Rome the Iberian horse was much sought after. Caesar himself was known to favour the white horses of Hispania. After the Moors were driven out of the Iberian Peninsula a gradual decline in the level of breeding took place but attempts were made in various European countries to preserve the line of the Spanish horses because of their suitability for High School riding. The Spanish horse was transplanted with success to Italy; Maximilian II introduced the Spanish horse into Austria in the 1560s, founding a Court stud at Kladrub, while his brother the Archduke Charles established a stud at Lipizza, near Trieste. These were the studs that supplied horses for the school in Vienna which thus became known as the Spanish School. Close collaboration and continual exchange of breeding stock existed between these two studs and a third one, Halpturn; the heavier type of horse bred at Kladrub was used for carriage work, while the

OPPOSITE AND ABOVE *Lipizzaner mares with their dark-coated foals in the paddocks of the Piber Stud. The whiteness is genetically dominant; some bays are produced but are no longer used in breeding.*

37

horses from Lipizza were kept for riding, in addition to some carriage work of a lighter nature. Over the years these horses with Arab and Barb blood in their veins, bred originally in the warm climate of Andalusia, proved to be endowed by nature not only with elegance of movement and regal bearing, but also with courage, hardiness and endurance.

Over the years some six lines were permeated, lines which have been used right down to the present day. These all trace back to the original Pluto (1765) a white stallion of pure Spanish descent, Conversano (1767) a black stallion of Neapolitan blood, Neapolitano (1790) likewise a Neapolitan, and a bay, Favory (1779) a dun from the stud of Kladrub, Maestoso (1819) a white stallion whose sire was Neapolitan and whose dam was Spanish, and Siglavy (1810) a pure white Arabian. In earlier centuries there were many blacks and browns, piebalds and skewbalds amongst the Lipizzaners but, since whiteness is genetically dominant, and since breeding for white in the emperor's official horses was strongly stressed, today it is the white horse which is associated with the name Lipizzaner. Bays are still produced – in conformity with genetic laws – but they are no longer used in breeding. The other foals are born brown, dark brown or mousey-grey and only acquire their snow-white coats by degrees over seven or eight years.

38

ABOVE *Work on the lunge rein in the Sommereitschule.*
OPPOSITE *In the stables of the Spanish Riding School.*

Austria

Because they are late developers the Lipizzaners have to be broken very carefully – particularly in the first year of their training. Some ten to twelve three-and-a-half-year-old stallions are selected for training each year and are brought from the stud at Piber to Vienna, where they are introduced for the first time to the saddle and bridle. The rest of that crop of foals are sold all over the world, there being a great demand for Lipizzaners because of their international fame and reputation.

The basic aim of the school is still to train first-class instructors, particular attention being devoted to the training of capable school riders who will be able, either at Vienna or elsewhere, to pass on their knowledge. A limited number of foreigners are accepted each year at the Spanish Riding School, the majority of them staying for a year, during which time they have the opportunity to acquire a very high standard of horsemanship and horsemastership. At all times particular emphasis is laid on the *whole* art of riding; riding must be considered as a whole, rather than as a series of specialised qualities, the whole, nevertheless, being divided into three types of horsemanship. The first stage involves riding in the most natural position with free forward movement – a style that can be developed by any competent rider. The second stage calls for riding with a collected horse, in perfect balance at all paces. Developed from the former, this is known as 'campaign' riding. In the third stage the horse is in an even more collected position, his highly flexible joints allowing him to display great agility and brilliance in all ordinary gaits, as well as in those unusual gaits and jumps sometimes performed by a horse when he is on his own in a field. This latter stage is known as the High School, but it cannot be developed without proper knowledge of the first two.

Obviously the training at Vienna is much more concentrated than at the ordinary riding school. This is because it is concerned with only one goal – the production of High School riding and High School performance. In Vienna there is neither cross-country riding, as there is at Saumur, nor jumping. The whole system in Vienna is geared towards the production of a very advanced High School horse, for nowhere is it more emphasised than in Vienna that a rider can only learn effectively on trained horses. If both horse and rider are beginners the rider is far less likely to acquire advanced knowledge. For this reason the pupils at Vienna, whether they are from outside or are school pupils

OPPOSITE *The passage or Spanish Walk*
OVERLEAF *The capriole in hand.*

who hope to become part of the school itself, are always put on fully trained horses, the training of the young horses being left to the most experienced instructors.

The exercises on the ground – that is to say the comparatively straightforward walk, trot, canter, shoulder-in, half-pass and eventually *piaffe* and *passage* (once known as 'the Spanish walk', it is still called the *Spanischer Tritt*, or 'Spanish gait' at the school) – are movements such as one might see in any good riding school in any country all over the world. It is in the movements 'above the ground' that Vienna is exceptional: these include the *courbette, levade, pesade* and *capriole*. In the *courbette* the horse executes several forward leaps on its hindquarters, without its forefeet ever touching the ground. In the *levade*, the horse lifts its forefeet off the ground, squatting on its haunches at an angle of up to forty-five degrees, maintaining this position for a length of time depending upon the horse's dexterity. The *pesade* is an extension of the *levade*. In the *capriole* the horse leaps simultaneously with all four feet and, at the height of its leap, body horizontal in the air, kicks violently back with its hind legs. It is, as has been said, frequently emphasised that these exercises of the classical school are based on the ordinary movements from nature such as may be seen when horses are playing or even, if they are stallions, fighting while out at grass. Based on these origins, these movements are then brought to perfection under saddle. The movements also date back to the times when horses were used in warfare, and many of them, it is claimed, were used originally in battle against an enemy. The classical school claims that it will not accept any unnatural movements, but there is an opinion today which feels that the exercises above the ground in the Spanish Riding School have become so stylised as to be unnatural and it is even suggested that in the foreseeable future they will be removed from the programme. It cannot be denied that for many people, although they admit the brilliance of these exercises above the ground, and although they accept that they should not be confused with certain not dissimilar circus movements, in the context of modern times they do, nevertheless, appear to be unnatural.

Many people visiting the Spanish Riding School in Vienna watch either the horses being schooled and/or the senior instructors working with their young pupils, but the greatest enjoyment of all comes from the

OPPOSITE *The school* quadrille; *the riders, immaculate in their brown tail-coats, cocked hats, high boots and white buckskin breeches, enter the riding hall.*

45

performance of the *quadrille*. This, indeed, *is* the Spanish Riding School of Vienna. The great school *quadrille*, lasting some twenty minutes and led traditionally by the commandant, is an unforgettable experience. Entering to the strains of Bizet's 'Arlésienne Suite', continuing to the music of Chopin and then in time to Ridinger for the canter, the superb finale is reached when the twelve perfectly matched white stallions work to the accompaniment of the music that they have used for nearly two hundred years – the 'Österreichischer Grenadiermarsch'. It is not only the excellence of the movements, the balance and the correctness of line that is so gripping, but the symmetry, the silent entry, the slow removal of their hats in salute; the beautifully maintained tack – the saddles and bridles gleaming – the immaculate double-breasted brown tail-coats, cocked hats, high boots, white buckskin breeches; the horses exquisitely groomed and in perfect condition. All this can never fail to bring a quickening of the pulse and, with the glorious music, frequently a lump to the throat. It is something that is quite unique, something that cannot be found anywhere else in the world – the complete consummation of the art of equitation.

It is sometimes said that today all this is an anachronism, but I would prefer to think that it is the height of equitation that acts as an inspiration and a target to which people involved in the training of horses all over the world can aspire. The standards maintained at Vienna are still as high as they ever were and Colonel Hans Handler follows in a distinguished line of commandants including the famous Colonel Alois Podhajsky who was his immediate predecessor. The discipline is strict, the training is hard, but the end result is something wholly memorable. One can truthfully say that such performance and such achievement wholly justifies the superb environment.

To appreciate Vienna in its proper perspective it is worth quoting Colonel Hans Handler's own thoughts on what the Spanish School is attempting to achieve.

'The level of dressage riding in a country is dependent on the instructor's ability and the quality of the horses available for the purpose. The broad basis of dressage riders, from which the best riders are picked for international requirements, is again dependent on the

OPPOSITE *The Commandant, Colonel Hans Handler, executes a* piaffe (above). *Movements 'above the ground':* the courbette *on the short hand rein* (right); *the* levade, *the length of time this position can be maintained is determined by the horse's dexterity* (far right).

46

number of good instructors and on the enthusiasm for this branch of sport. At the time of Pluvinel, Newcastle, de la Guérinière and Weyrother, dressage riding was part of the education of the young destined to support the state, of budding diplomats and field commanders, and it was, therefore, restricted to a well-defined layer of society. Nowadays dressage riding has become a type of sport which arouses more and more enthusiasm in all circles. It is a type of sport which can be carried on into old age and which has preserved the original idea of sport – that of *mens sana in corpore sano* – even in its maximum requirements.

'The International Dressage Judges Committee is responsible for the maintenance of the principles of classical dressage and for establishing the same definition in all countries. Dressage judges meet at congresses from time to time and hold discussions on the occasion of international competitions in order to try and ensure that mutually evolved ideas are also applied in practice. It would be of great benefit if chief instructors from each of the countries could be regularly called to attend meetings on an international level, meetings which would review the aims and the definition of the training of riders and horses. A mutual definition by instructors in all these matters would save their pupils disappointment on an international level and at the show ground and would prevent them from working in vain for years.

'The instructor must not only know the aims and methods of training, but must also be able to apply them practically; he must possess the experience that comes with long years of handling and training horses. He must himself be able to train horses to that level for which he feels himself to be qualified as an instructor. An instructor without a horse which he trained himself and on which his pupil can actually feel a correct *passage* or *piaffe* – something which cannot be explained in words – is like a football trainer without a ball. Apart from his training ability, the instructor must also have the ability to pass on knowledge: he must be able to teach. The weaker his ability for passing on his expertise, the more he needs a trained horse which may replace the instructor's deficiency by its own ability. The instructor must know what, know how, see, and be able to express his knowledge.

'He must know the principles of classical dressage and the aims of training in its consecutive phases up to the highest requirements, for

OPPOSITE *The quadrille. The pillars in the centre of the arena are used in teaching the exercises 'above the ground'.*

"he who does not know the goal cannot be on the right way" (freely translated from Morgenstern). He must convert theoretical knowledge into practice; he must know the ways and working methods with which to achieve the desired goal whilst caring for the horse as much as possible. He must be able to see, to recognise faulty behaviour and to find the causes which in most cases will not be found where they show up. He must have the ability of passing on this knowledge to his pupils as well.

'The classical art of riding develops the horse's natural gaits; if this art is properly applied, it promotes the psychological and physical development of the horse, schooling him for all types of riding except racing. Its aim is the unity of man and animal in harmony of movement; and its extreme perfection is High School. By the term High School of

50

equitation, we understand the ability of the horse – schooled by gymnastic training and the development of its mental capacity – to execute in perfect balance the most difficult movements; these are, however, in perfect harmony with the horse's natural gaits. The High School finds its expression in a deceptively playful ease and unison of movement.

'Exercises which are sometimes shown under the name of "High School" riding in circuses, such as a gallop on three legs or a Waltz step – things which are not the natural sequence of the foot fall in a walk, trot and canter – are out of place here. The classical school jumps or "schools above the ground" as they are called at the Spanish Riding School (the *levade, capriole* and *courbette*) are not in contradiction to this last principle. They are the result of sudden release from the utmost collection and can frequently be observed when young stallions play in the meadows.

'The training of the rider as well as that of the horse comprises two separate, but always closely connected lines. One aims at the development and promotion of potential physical characteristics in the human being as well as in the animal, and one is intended to develop fully the psychological talents of both. The training of the body is the aim of various doctrines of riding – that of the Spanish Riding School, as well as that of the school at Saumur among them. These techniques, tested over the centuries and tempered by solicitous care for the horses' legs, will lead to the ability to perform all movements, including those of the Olympic requirements, and will also ensure a long life for the horses.

'At a time when it appears possible to solve most problems with the aid of advanced technology, it is pleasant to find that the age-old experience of the riding masters still holds true: patience and hard work are the only effective tools. What Xenophon said in his Essay "About the Art of Riding" more than two thousand years ago and what has been frequently forgotten in the course of time, is to be asserted again to an increased extent: "The Gods have given man the gift of teaching man through words what they are to do, but it is obvious that one cannot teach a horse anything with words. However, if one rewards a horse each time it does what one wants of it and if it is punished when it is disobedient, it will best learn to do what it has to. Although all this is really idle theorising, it still gives the whole content of the Art of Riding."'

France

Saumur and the Cadre Noir

France

Saumur will always be associated with the legendary *Cadre Noir*. But what exactly is this élite group of brilliant riders and how did it achieve its name and renown?

Ever since the whole French cavalry was mounted, the *Cadre Noir* has formed the corps of equitation instructors for the cavalry school. With mechanisation this school has become the 'Armoured Corps School' in which the *Cadre Noir* has retained its role as instructors in the equestrian art. However, since 1 January 1969, because of cuts in the military budget, the *Cadre Noir* has been divorced from the school and even from the military. It now forms one of the two establishments of the National Institute of Equitation, a state organisation which is dependent upon three different ministries (Army, Agriculture, Youth and Sport) and which is responsible for co-ordinating riding in France in conjunction with the Fédération Française de Société Equestre. Though under a new administrative formula, the *Cadre Noir* is nevertheless the same institution which has dominated French equitation since 1814 – an institution whose fame has gone far beyond its own country's frontiers.

To understand the function, development and continuance today of the *Cadre Noir*, it is necessary to establish its place in the history of the French cavalry. Before the French Revolution the officers of the Royal Cavalry received their training at the famous School of Versailles, created in 1680 and established in the stables in front of Louis XIV's palace. Although renowned throughout Europe, the instruction given there was purely academic and formal and only partly suited to the demands put on mounted troops in battle. The School of Versailles disappeared with so much else at the time of the Revolution, and for some years there was nothing to take its place. Although the Empire used the Spanish cavalry in Russia at the turn of the nineteenth century, there were no longer the domestic facilities for the intense training of skilled riders that had existed earlier – an oversight which the Emperor himself realised for, among other things, it resulted in a great wastage of educated horses. So when Louis XVIII came to the throne in 1814, he re-established the tradition of Versailles in conjunction with more practical training. It was Saumur, where a cavalry school had existed since 1768, that he chose for his new project, no doubt remembering the time when he was still the Comte de Provence, brother of Louis XVI and honorary colonel of the heavy cavalry regiment which was garrisoned there.

The *Cadre Noir* has always been a select group of cavalry officers devoted to instruction. It was from the traditional uniform of the riding school of the cavalry – black with gold stripes and insignia – that the name *Cadre Noir* originated. The general military instructors of the school, whose uniform before the Second World War was a blue tunic, were called the *Cadre Bleu*. (The pretty ladies of Saumur, incidentally, were known as the *Cadre Rose*!)

Despite the many changes since 1969, this dashing group exists in its original form. It is composed as follows: under the direction of the *écuyer en chef* there are about ten *écuyers* (who at present are still officers) and ten *maîtres* and *sous-maîtres de manège* (at present non-commissioned officers). However, to these may be added, and no doubt will be, more *écuyers* and *sous-maîtres* recruited from among civilians and men who have left the army. The school has come full circle, for the new organisation reflects Saumur at the time of its founding when it was made up of both civilian and military elements.

The original *écuyers* responsible for instruction came from two sources. Some were civilians who had previously served at the School of Versailles and others were military personnel, officers from the regiments. Each group brought with it its own tradition: that of Versailles and its academic equitation on the one hand, and the tradition of military equitation based on the paces and exercises required for rugged cross-country riding on the other. It was this dual character – academic equitation allied to outdoor riding – which has distinguished Saumur throughout its entire history and in many ways still does so today.

Gradually the civilian elements were replaced by their military counterparts, although not without some unpleasantness. After repeated conflicts between the military and civilian factions the school was temporarily shut down in 1822 but it was again reopened in 1825 as a cavalry school. Despite this antagonism, towards the middle of the nineteenth century two civilians of unrivalled importance made their mark on the school. Comte d'Aure was appointed *écuyer en chef*. An enthusiast for cross-country riding and fast work, he introduced racing at Saumur and in 1852 an obstacle course called the Chemin Vert was laid out in

LEFT *Colonel de St André,* écuyer en chef *until 1972;* BELOW *A floodlit display by the* Cadre Noire.

the surrounding countryside. A veterinary corps to improve hygiene and the condition of the horses was also created. His influence was contrary to that of another most talented horseman, François Baucher. Unlike d'Aure, he had no experience of equitation in the field and, indeed, he is said to have never appeared out-of-doors. As a civilian Baucher chose for his arena the famous Cirque d'Eté, patronised by fashionable society. He brought new, erudite and revolutionary methods into dressage which he himself put into practice with remarkable talent. The authorities at Saumur were so impressed that they sent officers to study under him. However, his unorthodox methods could not be applied generally to the whole cavalry, being too sophisticated for a military milieu of average equestrian ability. Even Baucher admitted in his *Dictionnaire Raisonné d'Equitation* that it was difficult to put his ideas into words and the sharp spurs he promoted were not always successful when used by his pupils. In spite of the brilliant experiments within the army, neither Baucher nor his methods were finally accepted at Saumur.

Nevertheless, from 1840 to 1860 the military equestrian world was profoundly affected by this doctrinal struggle and it was not until the accession of Colonel l'Hotte (who had been the pupil of both masters in turn) to the post of *écuyer en chef*, that the two conceptions were merged into a method which took the best from both to form a suitable doctrine which successive *écuyers en chef* have faithfully passed down verbally to the present day – although their individual preferences may have inclined towards either d'Aure or Baucher at any one time. Colonel Dutilh (famed for 'lowering the horse's head and neck'), Colonel l'Hotte's successor, also assisted in this selective merging, as did Commandant de Montjou.

In the twentieth century, the indisputably talented Colonel Wattel reformed the school of equitation after the 1914–18 war (when the *écuyers* fought in the regiments), and the school went through a brilliant period right up to 1939, in particular under the instruction of Colonel Danloux (who was interested in modernising the method of riding over fences) and with the learned assistance of General Decarpentry. At this time Saumur turned its attention to sport: racing, polo and three-day eventing, without, however, forgetting the traditional *manège*. Dissolved again for the new campaign in 1939 the school survived in a

France

Lieutenant-Colonel Boisfleury, the present écuyer en chef, *leads the ride down the* Manège des Écuyers, *the indoor school made famous by the displays of the* Cadre Noir.

much reduced state at Tarbes and Fontainebleau from 1941–4. The *Cadre Noir*, once again at Saumur, was reorganised at the end of 1945 by Lieutenant-Colonel Margot and, in spite of great difficulties arising from military involvements in Indo-China and Algeria, it has carried on its rigorous training programme ever since.

Until 1969 the *Cadre Noir* had the controlling hand in the cavalry which was not restricted to the tradition of pure equitation of Versailles or Vienna, but which looked to the widest use of the horse. Under the close supervision of its officers both the student officers (lieutenants from the cadet school of St Cyr or student officers from the regiments) and potential instructor officers received daily training which later enabled them to instruct mounted troops and non-commissioned officers to ride across country, to go show jumping and to achieve a sufficiently high academic standard for cavalry purposes. At the same time an Equestrian Improvement Course was run specifically for officers so that after a ten-month course the most talented were able to specialise in events, horse shows and academic equitation. From among these men were selected the future *écuyers* of the *Cadre Noir*, as well as members of the international team under the command in turn of Colonel de Laissardière and Captain Bizard.

A course for student *sous-maîtres*, reserved for non-commissioned officers and lasting from three to nine months, enabled the numbers of *sous-maîtres* to be built up again after the wars, but this course was devoted to racing, cross-country riding, breaking-in and the *sauteurs* (airs above ground) speciality. Naturally the role of the *Cadre Noir* has changed since the cavalry was disbanded; this will be discussed later in the chapter.

What have remained in its original form are the collective displays of the *Cadre Noir*. While instruction in the basic equestrian skills constituted one part of the *Cadre*'s task, upholding by practical example the French doctrine of equitation has been of equal importance. This has been done in two ways: the *Cadre Noir* has given group displays and the riders have participated individually in all kinds of equestrian events.

The performances of the *Cadre Noir* are world famous and take two forms. The *écuyers*' performance, led by the *écuyer en chef*, lasts about twenty minutes. This consists of combined movements on one and two tracks, at the walk, trot and canter with changes of leg ending with the

passage. By tradition, the *écuyer en chef* executes certain refined movements, being the only one to show the school walk and the sustained trot. This display is known among the *écuyers* as the 'Black Mass' and is performed for the public at Saumur every Friday; it is also presented all over France and abroad.

In the *écuyers*' performance the riders use the old 'royal saddle' or 'pink saddle' favoured by de la Guérinière, and adapted from the saddle of the Middle Ages originally designed to enable the horseman to manage his mount with speed and precision. Made from white buckskin, it rests on a gold and purple saddle-cloth, accompanied by a black varnished leather bridle, gilded buckles and stirrups. It is extremely smart and effective. Their uniform is no less impressive: the *écuyers* wear a two-pointed hat, epaulettes and white breeches and carry a black and gold riding whip; their horses' manes are plaited with purple ribbons and bows. It is the privilege of the *écuyer en chef* to have a purple velvet saddle and his bridle is somewhat more ornate, the reins being woven in gold thread.

After this elegant display comes the even more colourful performance of the *sauteurs*. It is directed by a senior *écuyer*, followed by the youngest,

60

ABOVE *Some quiet schooling in the students'* manège *for the* écuyer en chef *and some of the student officers.*

ABOVE *The stable block; officers and civilian students receive instruction on the maintenance and care of their saddlery.* OVERLEAF *Some of the spectacular movements 'above the ground' of the* sauteurs.

and then by the *maîtres* and *sous-maîtres*. All wearing the same uniform, they use a white buckskin 'jousting saddle' which is the traditional saddle of the tournaments, in use until the seventeenth century. This saddle forms a sort of cradle from which the knights of the Middle Ages could resist the attack of an opponent. It is coupled with white leather equipment, the horses having their tails plaited and braided as in the past. Interestingly, the horses are not shod behind in order to avoid any danger of their shoes causing damage in the action of the jumps.

The *sauteurs* are not, of course, jumps over real obstacles but 'movements above the ground', derived from the 'school jumps' of the equitation of the past as exemplified in Vienna. These *sauteurs* were very much part of the great riding school repertoire of the seventeenth and eighteenth centuries established at most Courts, and include the *courbette*, the *croupade* and the *capriole*. The difficulty in this display consists particularly in the fact that the twelve riders must carry out *courbettes* and *croupades* together; only the more delicate *capriole* is done independently. The *sauteurs* have been purposely retained at Saumur, if deliberately modified under the influence of Colonel l'Hotte; to be well ridden they require both energy and tact on the part of the rider, two qualities which are necessary both in dressage and in riding over fences.

The Saumur Carousel or Tournament is held every year at the end of July. It is an equestrian and military festival – colourful, effective and highly varied in content – which is attended by several thousand spectators. The student officers put on a show lasting four days. A lance display, hurdle races and equestrian games (which include the *écuyers'* performance and *sauteurs*) are among the activities. The first of these tournaments was held in 1820 before the Duchesse de Berry and the school has faithfully carried on the annual tradition ever since, recently adding to the equestrian display a motorised show of exact precision.

The work of the *Cadre Noir* extends far beyond the world of High School displays. Officers of the *Cadre Noir* are an important part of many important international meetings. In dressage an *écuyer* has represented France at the Olympic Games in 1932, 1936, 1948 and 1952 when the two representatives included Colonel de St André, *écuyer en chef* until 1972. In horse trials two riders of the *Cadre Noir* formed part of the French team in Stockholm, Rome, Tokyo and Mexico – Guyon, the 1968 gold medallist, trained at Saumur and for ten years was a mem-

OPPOSITE *The* sauteurs *rehearsing their display. With the exception of the delicate* capriole, *the riders are required to execute all the movements in unison.*

65

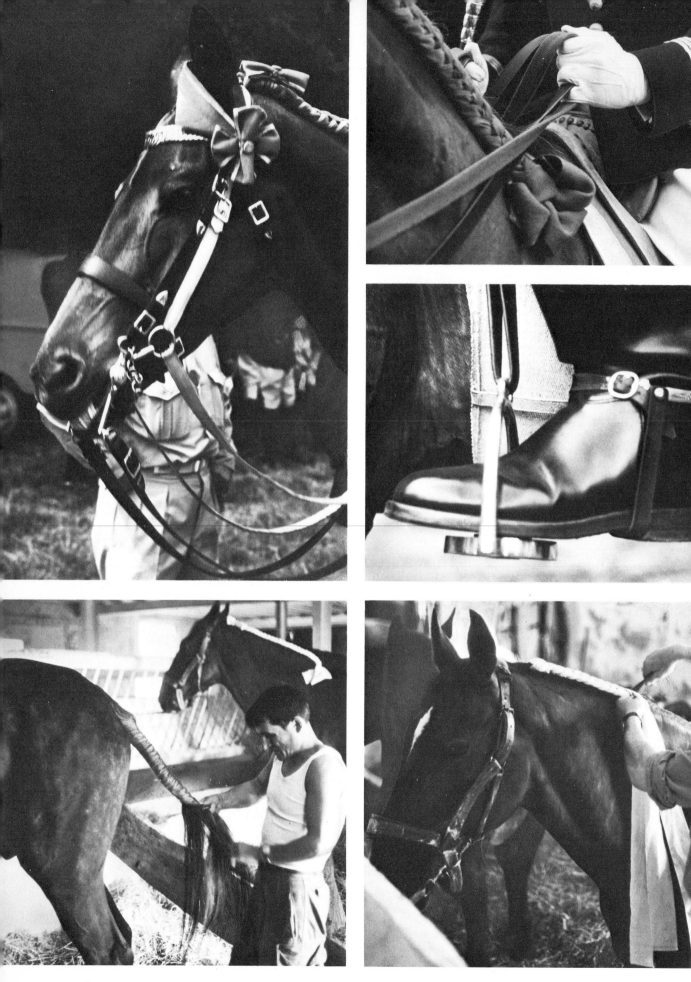

Preparation for a display. Horses and riders are turned out immaculately in keeping with the high standard of their performance.

ber of the *Cadre Noir*. His horse Pitou is now a show jumper ridden by Commandant Durand in international events. Saumur representatives have also distinguished themselves in show jumping and steeplechasing, illustrating their belief that the basic principles in riding apply to all its different forms.

Since 1969 Saumur has become the official Institut National d'Equitation. The *Cadre Noir* is the centre of it and in conjunction with the F.F.S.E. it does much to ensure that the famous spirit will be preserved and that the great tradition and expertise associated with Saumur for the past two hundred years will continue. The transitional stage during which the military establishment has developed into a national centre for the training of civilians has been carried out smoothly and efficiently. The role of the *Cadre Noir* has naturally changed under this new organisation and it is now the instructors of the overall committee, who teach the students and potential instructors. The *Cadre* acts as a consultant body, primarily concerned with perpetuating its own group and high standards, to whom the F.F.S.E. and E.A.A.B.C. can turn for advice and special training. It is still solely responsible for the Military Equestrian Course of the past, grouping together about ten officers or civilians, as will be more and more the case, for the purpose of supplying skilled riders to their own ranks. This is a regular nine-month course. Under the supervision of three instructors the officers first ride their novice dressage horse and their trained dressage horse alternatively. Then they work with their young and old show jumper or three-day eventer, each student being allocated four horses. There is an examination at the conclusion of the course for the Military Instructors' Certificate.

Maintaining the discipline and skill of those riders who have reached the ranks of the *Cadre Noir* requires no less detailed or rigorous a training programme. The *écuyer en chef* is responsible for the instruction of the *écuyers* for one hour each morning after which the *écuyers* work on their own. Again there are four horses for each officer. The *maîtres* and *sous-maîtres* also have four horses each. A senior *écuyer* assisted by the most senior *maître* is responsible for their training. In the morning they work with the event horses, in the afternoon they concentrate on the *sauteurs*.

For the civilian students the programme is rather different; a variable number of courses are held. The programmes are drawn up by the Office

OVERLEAF *Students learn to work their horses on the lunge.*

France

of Instruction, which is made up of two *écuyers* who check the progress and distribute the training facilities. This team deals with questions common to the *Cadre Noir* and the F.F.S.E., studying new methods and projects that could implement the training courses. Recently a video-tape machine and a tape-recorder were installed and have proved to be of great value.

The main course is that given for instructors. Twelve students of both sexes (some from overseas) are accepted on the condition that they hold the *Brevet de Moniteur* or have attained the status of assistant instructor. These courses start in October, and work for the Instructor's Certificate or *Brevet d'Instructeur d'Equitation* continues until July. The programme for this examination was originally planned by the F.F.S.E. Two *écuyers* and one *maître* start the training of these students and each day they use four horses, each adapted to a specific objective. The course is much the same as that given for the Military Instructors' Certificate, although in the latter case much less emphasis is placed on practical teaching.

IST HORSE IMPROVING THE SEAT AND BALANCE
1 Suppling up without stirrups
2 Use of cavalettis
3 Balancing work with stirrups
4 Jumping without reins

2ND HORSE THE AIDS
1 Two track work: shoulder in, half-pass, half-pirouette, rein back
2 Counter canter, changes of leg
3 Practice of dressage tests

3RD HORSE JUMPING INSTRUCTION
1 Work on the flat
2 Riding a single fence (uprights and spreads)
3 Learning to see the approach and take-off by going 'with' or 'against'
4 Learning to jump from an angle
5 Studying combinations and good and bad distances
6 Re-establishing distances with a long or short stride

Schooling on the lunge; the horse, while moving forward freely, should learn to bend to the line of a true nicrle.

France

4TH HORSE   PARTICIPATION IN COMPETITIONS
1   Daily preparation for the event (show jumping or event horse)

An important feature of the course is that each student is expected to teach a class, having prepared it in advance. At the end the other students discuss the class and the way it was conducted. In addition, there are conferences and lectures on teaching methods, the organisation of clubs and insurance. In the evenings there is first-aid practice, lectures on the practice and theory of horsemastership – and homework.

There are eight refresher courses held each year for instructors and assistant instructors, each lasting twelve days, for ten students. Again each student has four horses at his disposal and the course has three full-time instructors. Eight dressage courses for six students are held on very much the same lines. In addition to the four school horses, the dressage students are encouraged to bring their own horses.

The curriculum at Saumur is complemented by that of the Equestrian Centre at Fontainebleau, which runs courses for juniors, organises training in competitive riding for young people and also prepares students for the Assistant Instructor's Certificate. Both at Saumur and at Fontainebleau a large number of competitions are held – races, horse shows, horse trials, dressage and pentathlons.

The present set-up is impressive in the extreme and the E.A.A.B.C. is fortunate in the government support and encouragement it has received. Indeed France can claim one of the finest sites for its national centre. Designed as a military school in 1764, Saumur, on the left bank of the Loire, has grown to an attractive little town of twenty-five thousand inhabitants living in white houses with blue roofs stretching along the Loire. It is flanked by the Chardonnet, a large public park. Rising gracefully from the centre of the town is the castle, built between the eleventh century and the thirteenth, and remodelled in the sixteenth. The fourteenth-century town hall and many other medieval buildings are linked to the castle by ancient winding streets, bravely holding their own against the more modern parts of the town. At night the castle is floodlit and looks very romantic, reminiscent of the days when the young officers paraded the streets in search of the *Cadre Rose*. The castle itself now houses the Museum of the Horse.

The cavalry school (now, of course, devoted to armoured divisions)

An exercise to improve balance and develop an independent jumping seat.

stretches along the river on the south side, the centrepiece being an eighteenth-century building which looks out on to the parade ground, originally the old jousting ground. Formerly indoor riding schools and stables accommodating as many as two thousand horses surrounded the ground, but three of these are now used as gymnasiums and ordnance stores. Three indoor schools remain. The most famous of these, the *Manège des Écuyers*, still holds an indescribable aura which, one feels, can only bring out the best in a rider. It is here that the equestrian displays are given. There is stabling for 250 horses: a hundred for the *Cadre Noir*, a hundred for the training of students and fifty for civilian riders on short courses.

There are three open arenas or *manèges* for dressage or show jumping as well as two exercising grounds. Some five minutes away by horseback, along the Loire, is one of the two estates belonging to the school, Le Breil. Here is a show jumping arena, a cross-country course and a steeplechase gallop of five hundred metres. In the summer a small but very attractive thatched club-house at Le Breil is open for the students, with a lawn running down to the river. The larger of the two estates is at Verrie, not much further away. Four times the size of Le Breil, it consists of beautiful heath and forest, well drained and therefore suitable for any weather. Here too there is a steeplechase course on old turf, an eight-kilometre gallop, as well as a cross-country course with no less than five hundred jumps suited to either novice or more experienced event riders and horses.

The district is very definitely rural and agricultural, with prosperous farming and wine-growing. Interestingly one of its main products owes its very success to the horses. Three-quarters of the mushrooms grown in France come from this area, cultivated in large expanses of underground caves on layers and shelves of horse manure! It is alleged that the *Cadre Noir* itself survived economically during the difficult times of war only through this flourishing local industry. Not far from Saumur is the town of Angers where one of the national studs is housed, breeding Thoroughbreds, Arabs, Anglo-Arabs, trotters and many heavy French breeds.

The Saumur district is full of fascinating history. Even as far back as feudal times, a thousand years ago, the great castles of the Loire provided schools where the young nobility learned to ride. Famous tournaments took place in the Chardonnet, now comprising the parade ground, and

OPPOSITE *The training at Saumur combines the academic traditions of the famous school of Versailles on the one hand and the traditions of military equitation based on cross-country riding on the other.*

were attended by such dignitaries as the Plantagenet King Henry II, Charles VII and Saint Louis himself. Henry II and Richard the Lionheart were buried at the neighbouring Abbey of Fontevrault where Joan of Arc and the young Dauphin stayed with Charles VII's mother-in-law Yolande d'Anjou. Later Louis XIII and Marie de Medici were entertained at Saumur, and Louis XIV and Mazarin held Court there. With Louis concentrating on Versailles, Saumur suffered and the population dropped from 25,000 to 6,500. A new era opened for the area in the eighteenth century when it was chosen as the garrison town for the élite corps of cavalry, the Royal Carabinières.

So the great history of the school at Saumur began and since then many of the finest names in equitation have been associated with the school; moreover many men famous in recent French history have attended the school at one time or another: Leyautrey, Wegand, de Gaulle, Leclerc, Lattre de Tassigny, Lesage (an Olympic gold medallist) and America's General Patton and Britain's Colonel Sir Michael Ansell.

The present *écuyer en chef* carries on the great tradition, insisting on both hard work – the students ride five hours a day – and a proper balance of dressage and cross-country, always a tradition at Saumur. With the new opportunity to work in collaboration with the national trainers, the Marquis d'Orgeix and Monsieur Cochenet, he hopes to perfect the three disciplines: dressage, show jumping and cross-country.

There is great enthusiasm about the plans for the future, which include moving the whole school to Terrefort, just outside Saumur. After two years' deliberation, the financing of the plan has been approved and is fully backed by the government which appreciates the need for something that is imaginative and of high quality. Terrefort is a beautiful site of heath and forest land covering some 250 hectares including the present training area. There will be five separate units for instruction in the three disciplines and, of course, for the *Cadre Noir*. Each unit will have an indoor school with 120 stables; there will also be residential accommodation and all ancillary services including veterinary and farriery facilities. The whole plan will be completed by 1975.

'An organisation which does not look after its past has no future.' Under the *écuyer en chef* with the sustained tradition of Saumur and the *Cadre Noir* behind it, there can be little doubt that the school's future will be as glorious as its past.

OPPOSITE *Saumur: in the jumping lane, a young horse learns to jump boldly* (above); *two extensive cross-country courses have been built near the school* (below). OVERLEAF *An elegant display of perfect control, the* courbette *of the* Cadre Noir.

Switzerland

Reitsportzentrum Elgg

OPPOSITE *Paul Weier, who founded and runs the school at Elgg, has organised his own mounted brass-band there.*

Switzerland

I t is strange that Switzerland, a mountainous country that has seldom been involved in war, should be one of the last countries in Europe to lose its cavalry. As with other countries, the loss of the cavalry was to have a significant effect on riding in Switzerland, for just as the cavalry officers of Weedon in England and Saumur in France and the students of Caprilli in Italy played such a vital part in the development of equitation in their respective countries, so a tradition of riding in Switzerland had been largely dependent on the cavalry, right until the time of its disbandment within the last two decades. Although the Fédération Suisse de Société Equestre has played a major part in pursuing this tradition and generally improving standards, the progress of equitation – lacking, as it does, official government help – has not been easy since the cavalry was abolished. The old cavalry was an active body, comprising three full regiments with eighteen squadrons, each having 160 horses. Interestingly, every dragoon had to buy his own horse and keep it at home, bringing it to regular training sessions and equestrian contests. This led to a system of local 'riding clubs' with which Switzerland is now associated; in fact, many of the present clubs are firmly based on the cavalry foundations. These clubs, and the schools associated with them, are independent, organising meetings for all levels of riders – including those interested in competitive riding and dressage as well as juniors for whom specialised courses are set up.

The junior (aged sixteen and under) receives more attention than in many European countries. After taking part in regional competitions, young riders are grouped together during the off-season and someone appointed by the F.S.S.E. – either a top-class riding instructor or international rider – runs special courses at which an initial selection of those young riders with potential can be made. In the spring a central course takes place, usually at the Federal Army Horse Depot in Berne, and a second selection is made. The best of the young riders then receive permission to take part in higher courses, their progress being carefully watched by people appointed by the F.S.S.E. A final selection is made at a competition in mid-season and from this group the junior teams are formed. The team then undergoes intense training until it engages in international competition.

In addition to the F.S.S.E. training courses and competitions there are two special show jumping championships held in Switzerland – one in the French-speaking area and the other in the German-speaking area. They are organised by a journal which is chiefly concerned with horse affairs; these competitions are open only to those juniors who have won a sufficient number of points in designated competitions.

A somewhat similar scheme is run for riders who are interested in eventing; these riders meet in suitable areas where the ground lends itself to horse trials, for, understandably, it is not easy to find suitable areas for riding in Switzerland. Those riders who achieve success in the trials are then sent to compete in other European countries to gain experience. There are also courses for those interested in dressage – both juniors and seniors – which are organised by the F.S.S.E. Approximately a thousand juniors who have taken part in these various competitions are eligible for the special training. It should be emphasised, perhaps, that in addition to practical work there are written examinations on rules, regulations and basic knowledge of the horse.

There is a Swiss Association of Professional Instructors and Riding School Owners which for several years has organised these instruction programmes and examinations; this association has the patronage of the Swiss Department of Agriculture. The organisation is as follows: on leaving school, young people who are starting in the profession sign up for a three-year apprenticeship with an institution recognised by the association. Each institution has a riding master holding the Swiss diploma. During these three years apprentices from all over Switzerland are gathered once a year, for one week, to take courses organised by the Swiss Association of Professionals, so that there is some unity of doctrine. At the end of the three years a written and practical examination is taken at the Federal Stud of Avenches, which enables the candidates to obtain the title of groom, which can be awarded after only two years, or that of stable manager or apprentice instructor, which can be obtained only at the end of three years. If the students are prepared to do a further two years at a centre recognised by the association – either in Switzerland or abroad – they can then take a further examination with a more intensive practical side to obtain their second-class instructor's certificate.

At the end of these five years a candidate can choose to do a further two-year course in order to become a first-class instructor, taking an examination in which he is required to know all the disciplines thoroughly, or he can train at a recognised institution for the instructor's

OVERLEAF *Set in undulating grass country, untypical in Switzerland, Elgg is able to provide ample open space for cross-country work.*

diploma with final examinations which are spread over four weeks at the Federal Army Horse Depot at Berne. This final examination is usually taken at the age of twenty-five.

In recent years Switzerland has trained about fifty apprentices and ten grooms or stable managers. The first candidates for the instructor's examination (second-class) enrolled in 1972. Thirty riding instructors have now obtained their Swiss diplomas and are training apprentices in their own respective centres. In order to ensure a consistently high standard throughout the country there is an obligatory course held each year for such riding instructors. This is a very sound and imaginative policy.

Despite this there is some anxiety in Switzerland lest the Army depot may disappear in the same way as the cavalry. It is interesting that the vote of the people has twice saved the depot: something that one cannot easily imagine happening in any other country. In the event that the depot is closed, civilian centres are now ready to take over its responsibilities. Yet with all this activity on the instruction front there is no national school or national centre as such in Switzerland; but for some years Paul Weier, the well-known international rider, has run a school to which most international riders go for training and which, therefore, has become recognised as a school having an official, if not a national, status. This school is at Elgg near Zurich, and during the last decade it has acquired a very high reputation.

It is set in pleasant, undulating grass country with tree-clad hills in the distance – a very untypical landscape as far as Switzerland is concerned, which for the most part consists of its famous mountainous terrain. Obviously, even in this kind of country, there are not to be found hedges and ditches such as make the English Midlands or the Virginian estates a foxhunter's paradise. Nevertheless, it can be said to fulfil the English horseman's famous enquiry about a piece of country: 'It may be beautiful, but can you cross it?' In fact one can cross it, and it offers in addition most pleasant hacking amenities in the summer.

During the winter at Paul Weier's school there are training courses which are similar to the 'clinics' run in other countries – particularly in America and at Stoneleigh in England. These last only some two, three

86

OPPOSITE *Even the finest riders and most experienced horses go through what might be considered beginner's exercises which are invaluable in the development of the all-round carriage of horse and rider.*

Switzerland

or four days; the riders then go home, having learned their groundwork and having been given some 'homework' to keep them occupied during the next month. Returning a month later, having done their homework, their proficiency is fully tested. At the end of the winter Paul Weier holds a special indoor show. At this the riders are filmed, and their performances, as seen on the film, are later discussed in detail with a commentary and criticism by Paul Weier and other instructors.

Paul Weier, who was in the Swiss cavalry for ten years before retiring as a captain in 1959, was born in 1934. A versatile and imaginative person, he is interested and more than averagely competent in film-making, swimming and catering (he owns a local hostel). He is also a jazz and brass band enthusiast. He was Swiss National Dressage Champion from 1955 to 1957; in 1963, 1965 and 1966 he won the National Three-Day Event Championship; he created a record in 1969 by winning the National Show Jumping Championship for the sixth time, having won it first in 1959. It is unusual that he progressed from dressage to jumping and eventing instead of the other way round: frequently the more active riders take up dressage in their later years.

In 1969 he was responsible for the training of the Swiss Junior Team which won the European Junior Championships at Dinard. He rode Wolf with the Swiss Olympic team at Munich in 1972, when the team did very creditably, finishing fifth. He was also in the Rome, Tokyo and Mexico teams. His other well-known horse was Wildfeuer. His major successes as a rider also include the Grand Prix in Rome (1966), the Grand Prix in Lucerne (1970) and the Grand Prix in Lisbon (1971). He is fortunate that in 1972 he married a woman as passionately interested in equestrian affairs as himself – Monika Bachmann, who has ridden in two Olympic Games and is regarded as one of the most successful lady riders in the world. She herself won the Grand Prix in Lisbon in 1969 on her best-known horse, Erbach. The courses that they run at Elgg could be described as a mixture of the best of the Germanic style, with its precision and control, and the elegant fluency of the American riders as trained at Gladstone by Bertalan de Nemethy; in fact, the great trainer of the United States team was himself an instructor in Switzerland some twenty years ago.

Obviously in a country such as Switzerland, with its severe winter conditions and its mountainous terrain, riders encounter special

OPPOSITE *Elgg: in style the Swiss combine the precision and control of the Germans with the elegant fluency of the Americans. Most of their horses are imported and are carefully selected to suit their training methods.*

TOP *Using a video-tape machine, Paul Weier records a pupil's performance for detailed analysis afterwards.*
ABOVE *Weier places great emphasis on the physical well-being of his students. After a day's hard work, the students report to the gymnasium to be put through their paces.*
OPPOSITE *Course-building in miniature; Paul Weier prepares a new test for the students.*

Working on the lunge without reins and stirrups, perfecting the balance and seat of the rider.

difficulties in training and working horses. In the winter months it is difficult to work them out of doors at all. Considerable emphasis, therefore, is placed on training and riding in indoor schools. When Paul Weier started his school in 1964, he had only one small indoor school, but a new and very impressive school was built in 1972, measuring thirty by seventy metres; this has greatly increased the scope for work at Elgg, especially indoors where some fifty or sixty horses are kept – some owned by their riders who keep their horses at the school, and some belonging to the school itself. Paul and Monika Weier have some fifteen to twenty top-class show jumpers themselves, while many of those horses belonging to others are of international standard. Few horses are specially bred in Switzerland, most of them being imported from Ireland, England, Germany and France. It is possible, therefore, to be selective in the horses that are trained.

The Swiss show jumping team meets at Elgg twenty-four times a year, with special preparation before the big shows such as Aachen and, of course, before the European Championships, the World Championships or the Olympic Games. The other big shows on which they concentrate are their own national shows at Lucerne, Geneva, St Gallen, and Davos where they jump on the snow. The training in the indoor school is aimed at concentrating on the work on the ground: in other words, dressage. Paul Weier's mother was a well-known dressage

enthusiast and originally his parents ran the school at Elgg on classical lines with an instructor, Major Oscar Franck, who had an international reputation. From this it will be seen that Weier, in common with most leading riders and instructors today, appreciates the importance of dressage as a vital part in the training of a show jumper.

Although there are special dressage courses at Elgg, it is on jumping that the principal efforts of the school are ultimately concentrated. It is fortunate for Swiss equitation that a man of Weier's stature should be available, for he possesses advanced but carefully considered theories and is determined to improve standards throughout. He feels that there is still room for much improvement in the kind of courses and fences built for show jumping in Switzerland, and it is due to his efforts and example that Swiss riders more frequently visit other countries to take part in international shows – anxious and willing to learn something from the different competitions and courses.

Despite the difficulties of the terrain, eventing is becoming increasingly popular in Switzerland, and at Paul Weier's school he has a course of permanent fences, ditches, walls and banks. In addition, at Frauenfeld, some twenty kilometres from Elgg, there is a racecourse with forty or fifty natural fences forming an excellent cross-country course for eventing: it is here that the Swiss Fédération runs its own one- and two-day events.

Lodging for those participating in school programmes is managed in a highly original way: in conjunction with the riding school the Weiers are

Switzerland

Acrobatics in the saddle while practising for display work.

responsible for a delightfully comfortable old inn built right on the village street. Elgg itself is not a particularly beautiful village, but it has an engaging atmosphere, and those taking part in the courses are happy to stay in this cosy and welcoming environment.

Although the focus at Elgg is primarily on show jumping, it is in the sphere of dressage that the greatest interest has been shown in Switzerland. Today very nearly one hundred official dressage shows and events are held each year, this number having almost doubled in the last three or four years. It is interesting to recall that in all official events a simple dressage test is often included for the jumpers, and sometimes this is obligatory. The Swiss have been helped in achieving a uniformity of doctrine by the invitation issued by the F.S.S.E. to General Niemack to run special courses for dressage judges. Those attending these courses

94

go on to hold courses for dressage riders in their own cantons: thus standards are perpetuated.

It is the main target of all these dressage events to produce people sufficiently good to compete abroad. Nevertheless, despite the improvement there are as yet, according to the Fédération's annual report, only a limited number of riders who can be regarded as of top international calibre. It is felt that there is still a long way to go. As there is no government assistance, it is not easy to ensure the progress that the enthusiasm deserves but, thanks to the great and sustained efforts of the leading members of the F.S.S.E., gradual progress is being achieved and already the performances of Swiss riders in international competitions are of a noticeably higher standard than a few years ago. In a bold step the Fédération has recently acquired the services of a riding master

ABOVE *After a training session the horse is allowed to roll free in the indoor school.*

from the Spanish Riding School of Vienna who has taken charge of the training of the more promising dressage riders.

Already, as in Sweden and Germany, courses for grooms are held in Switzerland with the goal of improving the standard of horsemastership throughout the country. Pay for grooms, however, is low but, as in other countries, the pay and status of those who work in stables is improving.

The state of equitation in Switzerland today is very encouraging for a small country which inevitably suffers from lack of amenities. Nevertheless, it cannot be denied that it is sad for a country that kept its cavalry going so much longer than any other country in Europe – even though the total cost of the cavalry was equal to the cost of one Mirage Fighter – not to have more government assistance. It would be of inestimable value to the Fédération to have a nationally sponsored or subsidised centre. Switzerland is indeed fortunate in the school run by Paul and Monika Weier at Elgg, for it is filling a very vital gap, and sustaining the momentum of progress in the various fields of equitation.

OPPOSITE *The principal efforts of the school are ultimately concentrated on preparation for the show jumping arena and the Swiss show jumping team meets regularly at Elgg to prepare for the major events of the season. Work out of doors is limited by severe winter conditions but a course of permanent fences has been built for additional preparation.*

Sweden

*Ridskolan
Strömsholm*

Sweden

Literally translated, Strömsholm means 'an island between two streams' and the castle of this name built in 1558 for King Gustaf Vasa is indeed on its own small island. But the history of Strömsholm reaches back still earlier to the year 1521 when this same king established a stud on the island. Since that time there have been many changes but a tradition of equestrianism remains strong.

In 1630 King Gustavus Adolphus gave the castle to Queen Maria-Eleonora; in 1654 King Charles x presented it as a wedding gift to his wife Queen Hedvig-Eleonora, who kept it for sixty years. Her monogram can still be seen over the main entrance: H.E.R.S., standing for Hedvig-Eleonora Regina Suedia or, as it has been translated by generations of students, 'Hellish Elegant Riding School'. Hedvig-Eleonora had the castle almost completely rebuilt in 1681 and it is the same today.

The nineteenth century saw many innovations. The stud became a stallion depot in 1887 and remained as such until the 1950s. The Army Riding and Equitation School was founded in 1868, remaining at Strömsholm for exactly a century until it was closed down in 1968. Since then Strömsholm has followed the example of other schools, and the once flourishing cavalry has given way to a civilian riding and equitation school administered in Sweden by the Ridfrämjandet (Swedish Equestrian Federation) and the Svenska Ridsportens Central Förbund (Swedish Horse Society). The school is situated 120 kilometres west of Stockholm on the north coast of Lake Mälaren. The nearest village is Kolbäck, about a ten-minute drive away, and the nearest major town is the industrial centre of Västeras.

Since the school passed into civilian hands, the director has been Hans Ernmark who is also the Secretary General of both the Swedish Horse Society and the Swedish Equestrian Federation. Surprisingly enough, Hans Ernmark was never in the Swedish cavalry, nor has he taken part in any competitive riding. Nevertheless, he has always been interested in horses, having ridden since he was five or six. Born in 1916, he later qualified as an economist and engineer at the Swedish University in Stockholm. An adept organiser and administrator, he was in the department-store business for twenty-five years. Eventually he decided to retire from business and devote himself whole-heartedly to equestrianism. On 1 January 1962 he was appointed Secretary General

PREVIOUS PAGES *The instructors and students of the Ridskolan Strömsholm.*

to both societies, taking over the directorship of the riding school at Strömsholm in 1968. The policy, and it seems to be a wise one, was to appoint a good civilian administrator rather than a cavalry officer. He is very much helped in his work by his wife Marianne, who is his assistant. For many years she has taken part in dressage competitions and is now an international judge of high repute. Their daughter, a keen show jumper, had one season competing at international shows. The family farm is at Södertälge within easy access of the riding school.

Ernmark has tremendous enthusiasm for everything connected with the horse, which he instils into all who work with him. He is respected by all the staff at Strömsholm, always having a word for everyone, from the man sweeping up the stables to the woman working in the kitchens. Although his main responsibility is for administration, he enjoys lecturing to the students as it is in this way that he can get to know them better. Many past students come back to renew old acquaintances which in itself speaks well of the atmosphere.

The head of the school and chief instructor is Major Hans Wikne, an ex-cavalry officer who first received instruction at the Spanish Riding School in Vienna and later went to Strömsholm as a student. He re-

ABOVE *The castle of Strömsholm, built in 1558, is now a museum. Directly behind the castle is the main show jumping arena and stretching away into the distance the racecourse, the home of the Swedish Grand National.*

Göran Casparsson in the jumping arena.

mained for ten years as senior dressage instructor until his retirement from the army in 1962. In 1968 he became the national instructor and as such he is responsible for organising all the courses, instructing only basic riding and dressage. His duties also entail travelling all over the country arranging courses for dressage judges and follow-up courses for the leading riders – as well as inspecting riding schools. He is now sixty and has been associated with Strömsholm for twenty years. Göran Casparsson, aged forty-two, is the instructor for show jumping and combined training. He has been at the school for five years and has had previous experience as the head of various other riding schools. His father was a member of the gold medal winning team in the three-day event at the Olympic Games in Stockholm in 1912, the first of the modern Olympics. Göran himself has jumped successfully at the national level.

Riding in Sweden is obviously very much on the increase, and there, unlike many countries, it is a sport which ordinary working people take part in – it is not just top executives who own horses. There are now some sixty thousand members of the Swedish Horse Society. Membership has doubled in the past few years and there is a twenty per cent increase in membership each year. Approximately fifty per cent of the riding population are members. Statistics indicate that of all the riders, ninety per cent are under twenty-four years of age, and eighty per cent are girls! There are some thirty-five thousand riding horses and ponies in Sweden making a total of sixty-five thousand with trotters and racehorses.

Despite this soaring popularity there is astonishingly little incentive to compete. Riding is very much for pleasure and leisure rather than for competition. Indeed there are only twenty national shows a year at which show jumping competitions are held. The reasons are manifold: although nearly all horses are home bred, very few people own more than one horse as the upkeep is so expensive; there is no sponsorship as we know it so the financial burden on an international rider – who must have several horses in order to compete – is very great. Jan Wannius is probably the most successful Swedish show jumper; his father, a well-known official in Swedish riding circles, paid for a complete season's jumping. Competing nationally and internationally with three or four horses, he was able to recoup only about £1,200 ($3,000).

Currently there are about 178 riding clubs in Sweden. Up till now amateur instructors have filled the needs of these organisations, but obviously with more and more riders, professional instructors are preferred. It is to Strömsholm that riders must look for these instructors.

Every facet of riding and horsemanship is catered for at Strömsholm. Apart from the main instructors there are saddlers, farriers and a veterinary surgeon in permanent attendance. The senior farrier, stable manager and vet all give lectures in their area of specialisation; the vet also gives some riding instruction.

The area where the school is situated comprises five hundred acres of open land although there is also woodland which can be used for riding. Included in this area is the racecourse where the Swedish Grand National is held. The heart of the school, the castle, still belongs to the

king. Once the mess for the cavalry, it now serves as a museum. The remainder of the estate belongs to the state, to which an annual rent is payable of over £15,000 ($37,000). It is rented only on a yearly basis as the government is not at present prepared to grant a long lease.

The main school buildings form a large hollow square with stable blocks on two sides. Running down the centre of each is a long passage flanked by stalls and some looseboxes. Each block houses sixty horses with facilities for food stores and rest-rooms for the staff. The stables are very warm, an important feature in view of the rugged winters, and the standard of stable management is very high. There is yet another building where an additional twenty horses may be stabled during the summer. There are approximately sixty permanent school horses.

At either end of the complex are riding halls. The smallest is forty by twenty metres and is used for schooling young horses. Attached to it is a place for driving vehicles. Just under a mile away is the old cavalry school commander's house which is now used as an office block and conference centre with excellent accommodation for students.

Opposite the training school is a very imposing building designated for dressage with a jumping hall next door. Both of these are eighty by thirty-five metres. The jumping hall has been ingeniously fitted out with a steel frame on pulleys which can be raised or lowered easily, giving a free jumping lane right round the school. The entrance to each hall is neatly placed at the end where there are small galleries and a jump store.

Behind these two main riding halls are the saddlers' and farriery block; lecture rooms seating as many as fifty people; housing for permanent staff; a coffee shop where students and staff can meet; a mess block with dining-room and a kitchen together with a reception room where VIPs may be entertained. (For the most part the catering, done by an outside firm, harkens back to the old days of the military canteen.) There are two bungalow-type blocks for student accommodation where each student has a separate room with a wash basin. There is a central area with toilets, baths and showers. Seventy-five to eighty students can be housed. Altogether there are fifty single rooms but a further hundred riders can be put up in dormitories while shows are in progress and there is unlimited space for caravans and tents. If the load is too much, there are three towns within a twenty-mile radius with good hotels.

OPPOSITE *From 1868 to 1968 Strömsholm housed the Army Riding and Equitation School* (above). *Sixty horses can be stabled in each of the two main stable blocks and in view of the severe winters heating is an important feature* (below).

Sweden

There is a vast area where one can ride, and numerous cross-country obstacles. Close to the main area there is a small outside arena for use during the summer months. The main show jumping arena is two hundred by sixty metres, situated immediately behind the castle. It has a permanent water jump, some small waters, a bank and permanent hedges. Beyond the ring is an international-size dressage arena. There are smaller dressage arenas as well.

Although the school is essentially a national centre, students from other Scandinavian countries are welcome, as are students from other parts of the world – from beginners to advanced, including ex-cavalry officers. From 1 June 1972 to 31 May 1973 some 522 students attended courses at Strömsholm, making a total of 9,171 student days.

The basis of all the riding courses is a thorough knowledge of dressage. The main courses are the three parts of the riding instructors' course, the aim of which is to produce straightforward, competent, knowledgable horsemen. There are often three courses running at the same time (RIK I and II and a ten-week course for grooms, for instance).

ABOVE *In the paddocks at Strömsholm; the jumping hall beyond.*
OPPOSITE *The indoor school at Strömsholm with its impressive arched timber roof.*
Major Hans Wilkne instructing.

Numerous cross-country obstacles have been erected across the pleasantly wooded acres.

For Part I of the instructors' course, a potential student has to be aged nineteen or over. He attends an eight-week course and then goes to another riding school for one year, returning to complete Part II – a six-week course. If he wants to be a director of a riding school, he stays for Part III, which necessitates 180 days or six months in residence at Strömsholm. At the end of this he takes part in competitions at the school and is allowed to enter the Malmö Show. If a student is to be an authorised riding instructor – fit to run a riding school or look after a district – he must be over twenty-three by the time the course is completed. The best student of the year is always invited to stay on another year in order to ride the top dressage horses.

In order to attend the RIK course, a student must have had five years' riding experience and six months' instruction under a qualified instructor. He must also have taken a two-month further education course including economics and veterinary science. Students who wish to receive instruction, but not to instruct, may attend these courses, but they must complete each course they start: i.e., if they go on Part II they must stay for the whole six weeks.

OPPOSITE *Strömsholm: a great sense of friendship and co-operation involves everyone at the school and a real sense of eager enthusiasm is evident among the students.*

Students may bring their own horses which will be used only if they are thought suitable. In any case, each student has to look after and ride three or four other horses. If his own horse is not formally assigned to him, he must take care of the horse in his spare time. The student's day starts at 7.30 am and finishes at 5 pm, with a break for lunch from 11.30 to 1.00. Usually the students are free in the evening, though sometimes there are lectures.

Although more than 150 riders apply each year for RIK I, only fifty are admitted; thirty-six take Part II, and approximately ten take Part III. For the riding courses the cost is £12 ($30) per day, payable by the student. This is wholly inclusive. RIK I and II courses cost private students £240 ($600) while the army, police and overseas students pay £500 ($1,250). The advanced course, RIK III, costs twice this amount.

One aspect of the curriculum at Strömsholm that is particularly interesting is the addition of courses in driving for both two- and four-horse vehicles. As Hans Ernmark says, with the present fuel problems, people are taking a greater interest in driving. He hopes very much that Sweden will shortly be able to compete internationally in this sport.

The whole organisation at Strömsholm is very impressive: there is a great sense of friendship and co-operation between everybody, and the students, though well-disciplined and immaculately turned out, are not rigid but constantly stimulate a real sense of urgency and enthusiasm. The calibre and importance of the school are reflected in the fact that all Swedish Olympic medallists in the past have passed through Strömsholm at some stage in their lives, for either short or long courses. (The one exception, strangely, is Jan Jonsson, the bronze medallist in Munich. At the time he was an NCO there were no courses available to him.)

One hopes that Strömsholm will continue to be able to meet the growing demands, that it will expand and introduce such refinements as video-tape machines and other training aids. As it is the whole place is summed up best, perhaps, by Anders Gernandt, the well-known Swedish television commentator, who said, 'It is one of the most charming places in Sweden, and a paradise for horsemen.'

Ernmark, who is unashamedly ambitious and always forward-looking, would be the first to agree with Anders Gernandt, and he would like

Winter in the grounds of Strömsholm.

to see the facilities made available to more people. As he himself says: 'I am most anxious as soon as possible to increase the number of horses, the number of instructors, the number of riding arenas, so that we can then increase the number of students. At present fifty attend the elementary course. This should be at least 150. I have no doubt whatever that the present increases in attendance will be continued. In seven years I hope to double the numbers.'

Hans Ernmark wants very much for Strömsholm to be known not as a riding school, but as the Swedish University of the Horse. Negotiations are in fact being carried out with the Department of Education in the hope that the department will take over the costs of the school. As it stands now, finances for sport in Sweden are administered by the Riksidvotts-Förbundet – the Central Sports Organisation – which receives about £6 million ($15 million) each year from the Department of Agriculture to be divided among all the sports as they see fit. All money received by the horse societies goes into the running of Strömsholm rather than into providing facilities for competition and international travel. If these negotiations with the Department of Education are successful, then nation-wide facilities can be improved and the number of students increased, particularly that of the advanced students and those wishing to become instructors. With the energetic, resourceful and imaginative Hans Ernmark in command there is little doubt that Strömsholm will soon justify the title of university.

It seems likely, too, that as a result of these plans Sweden will once again attain its rightful place in the world of the horse. The military school at Strömsholm lasted exactly one hundred years and succeeded in producing successful Swedish riders to represent their country in the Olympic Games and other international events. In fact, between 1912 and 1928 Sweden won more Olympic medals in the equestrian events than any other nation. Names such as Lewenhaupt, von Rosen, Sandstrom, Laudstron, Svensson, St Cyr and Blixen-Finecke are all part of equestrian history.

Hans Ernmark emphasises repeatedly that today dressage must be the basis for the education of the horse and rider as it was in the past. One of the reasons, originally, for establishing the riding school at Strömsholm was to maintain the old tradition of Klas Adam

OPPOSITE *Riding is very much a pleasure sport in Sweden and professional racing is popular (above). Over five hundred students attend courses at Strömsholm each year; although essentially a national centre, students from all parts of the world are welcomed (below).*

Sweden

Ehrengranet, known as the Pluvinel of Sweden. His principles are inscribed round the wide riding hall at Strömsholm:

> True art never grows old.
> Where the art goes out, force comes in.
> To mastership there is only one way
> Like the way of the sun in a blue sky:
> To aim upwards and reach for the supreme
> Yet never to think oneself master.

(A literal translation of a verse that rhymes and scans in Swedish.)

Ernmark follows an illustrious line of predecessors such as Fischerstrom and Nyblaeus. He is not a horseman of their calibre, but his administrative ability may in the long run prove to be of no less value to Strömsholm.

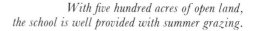

With five hundred acres of open land,
the school is well provided with summer grazing.

LEFT *The emblem of the Burevestnik Riding Club.* BELOW *Schools such as Burevestnik produce most of Russia's top equestrian competitors. Alexander Sokolov, a Master of Sport from the Burevestnik Society.*

USSR

The fact that many people in their childhood thought of Russia only in terms of Cossack riders whom they saw at circuses and horse shows makes one realise that Russia has always been identified with horsemanship; yet of all the countries in Europe it has probably been most difficult for Russia, ravaged by revolution and two world wars, to establish a continuous tradition of equestrianism.

In fact, more than fifty thousand people ride regularly in Russia today, although this is still a relatively small number when compared with such countries as the United States, Germany, Britain and France. Nevertheless, each year some thirty important competitions are staged to establish the champion rider of the USSR; indeed, there are many famous Russian riders today, such as Shabailo, Boris Lilov, Lev Baklishkin, Boris Konkov, Saboital Mursalimov, Tatiana Kulikovskaya, Sergei Filatov, Ivan Kalita, Carl Brodaski and Nicolas Mikhailov.

But the early days were extremely difficult. For at least a decade after the Revolution there was no organised riding in Russia other than in the cavalry regiments, but it was eventually due to the Board of the Revolutionary Military Soviet that riding was brought back into the popular arena. Until the mid-twenties riding was considered a purely military art. In 1925 the Central Equestrian Committee, whose motto was 'Riding – one of the basic aspects of military preparedness is the cavalry' held the first all-Union competition. The events, however, were very much geared to the demands of the military.

At this time Marshal Budyonny was in charge of the military equestrian section and it was he who first determined that riding facilities should once again be accessible to civilians. Consequently he assumed control of Ocoaviaxim – a project designed to promote the development of the art of riding on a wider basis than before. Eventually, in the mid-thirties, the Committee for Sport and Physical Culture took over the responsibility for equestrianism, and riding was finally divorced from the military. The Committee for Sport and Physical Culture, somewhat similar to the Sports Committee in other countries, is the overseer for all sports societies and is, of course, a branch of the government. All sports, therefore, are subsidised, although the amount of the subsidy has always varied depending on the funds available. The funds have to go round more than forty sports societies, many of them specifically linked with one or other of the professions. Each sports society has its own local clubs.

One such society is Burevestnik, and its Moscow branch is one of the main equestrian centres in the USSR.

But it has taken many years for Russian equestrianism to reach this stage. Originally, back in the mid-thirties, two clubs were set up in Moscow – each associated with trade unions: Spartak and Stroitel. The latter – and the word means 'Builder' – is the forerunner of the Burevestnik Society. It is remarkable that these two original clubs were ever able to get off the ground, considering the tremendous odds against them. The Stroitel Club, parent of the Burevestnik Society as it were, took shape on the edge of Izmailova Park where there was a cavalry station. The very fine site, surrounded by lush stretches of greenery and woodland, is situated near the entrance to the park, but the only building available at the time it all started was a kind of summerhouse. The land and the building were made available to Budyonny's Ocoaviaxim project in order that a cavalry station might exist for hiring out horses.

In a comparatively short time, however, the summerhouse was refurbished and improved as much as was practicable, and ten horses, four of which were draught horses and all of which were army cast-offs, were given to these early pioneers. Funds, however, were desperately short and the only way the club could raise a little capital to expand its modest beginnings was to hire out the draught horses. Surprisingly perhaps to the pioneers – but not so surprising in retrospect – people from different walks of life joined the club, enthusiastically rolling up their sleeves in preparation for the hard work ahead, for it was the members who contributed much of the labour needed to build the school. The main working force behind the club was the Engineering, Construction and Architecture Institute. They seemed anxious to develop and expand the shed. Korshev, a well-known architect, played a leading part, taking a sympathetic approach to the site's possibilities, and devising a series of trails and tracks through the woods. Most important of all, he designed the stables which were completed before the end of the 1930s. As soon as the stables were completed, the two Moscow Clubs, Spartak and Stroitel, took part in a competition held in Rostov-on-Don. In 1937 another riding club was formed in Moscow; this one was connected with the food industry and its trade union. In 1938 Stroitel acquired its first Thoroughbred horses; this was a turning point for the school which, up to this time, had been entirely dependent

on military cast-offs. The school now felt that it was in a position to begin to train riders and horses *together* – the beginning of their typically technical and scientific attitude towards training.

Then the war came, and even more than in most European countries, the result for equestrianism, in particular for the riding schools, in Russia was disastrous. All the horses were drafted into the army, the school was turned into a military station for defence and anti-aircraft purposes; deep ditches scarred the park. Most unfortunate of all was the fact that many of the instructors and riders who went to the war never returned. The whole site was in a sorry state. The school had to start completely from scratch, and once again it was faced with desperate lack of financial means. But this time, more than ten years since the original school had come into being, the demands were much greater because the members' technique was more advanced, the approach to equestrianism more sophisticated. They wanted to raise enough money to construct a *manège*, an exhibition area with seating accommodation, stables and all the necessary subsidiary buildings. It was not until the end of 1948 that it was possible to begin to implement any of these plans.

As the demands for more advanced training and sports facilities grew, the original organisations found themselves unable to cope. Consequently there was a general reshuffling of the sports clubs. Stroitel became part of the Voluntary Sports Society, Nauka (Study), which included the universities. There was enormous support from the students' sector whose skill and expertise brought them repeated success in the All-Union competitions. Their achievements during this period are particularly remarkable when one appreciates that, as they did not have a *manège* of their own, they had to borrow the facilities of another club from 10 pm until midnight!

With time what we recognise as the Burevestnik Society grew out of Nauka. Burevestnik is today a club almost exclusively for university students – particularly engineers, geologists, biologists and veterinary surgeons. It is unfortunate that, owing to the enormous demand for places at the Burevestnik Riding Club, it is necessary to be highly selective. There are insufficient vacancies for more than a handful of ordinary members, the majority of the members all being students with a future that is directly or indirectly connected with horses and riding.

OPPOSITE *Viktor Matveyev, twice USSR champion. Soviet riders are able to gain valuable experience in preparation for international competitions in the Spatakiada, the sports competitions held annually in the USSR, and in which, since they restarted after the war, riding has played a major role.*

Obviously riding for these people has to take second place to study, but the training is so rigorous that those who do show talent stand a very good chance of being considered for international events; far more so, obviously, than the person who just pays his rouble at the local hippodrome for forty-five minutes in a paddock or on the roads and tracks with a dozen or so other riders. The fortunate and talented ones can also train to become instructors and horsemasters.

It is now over twenty years since the first buildings of Nauka were completed, with seventy looseboxes, an arena 180 by seventy metres, with audience accommodation, and another arena of sixty by twenty metres which was added later. It was in 1955 that Burevestnik finally came into existence as it is known today, the students virtually taking over in a voluntary manner. The outstanding student at this time, and a considerable influence in the take-over, was Eliseev, who contributed greatly to the growth of popularity of riding, and the improvement in the standard of riding in Russia. Nevertheless the presiding genius at Burevestnik almost since its inception is Mikhail Sergei Ivanov.

At this time solidarity was developing within the Soviet Union. Moscow, as the capital and the most established equestrian centre in the country, encouraged the development of riding in the new republics.

Mikhail Sergei Ivanov, the presiding genius behind Burevestnik.

Burevestnik established particularly close links with the new republic of Estonia, and a long-standing friendship and spirit of co-operation grew up between the clubs. Seminars were held where the leading members met to discuss new methods of training and breeding. Above all the clubs pooled their precious resources and in many instances they competed as one team in the early competitions.

Not altogether surprisingly competitions play an important part in the riding world in Russia. This is partially due to the scientific attitude Russians take towards their sports, so that achievement and results are all-important. The sports societies responded immediately to the introduction of competitive riding. The interest was such that when the Spartakiada of the USSR was held for the first time after the war in 1965 not only were funds designated for a large equestrian arena at Luzhniki, but riding played a major role in the whole affair.

There are competitions in dressage, show jumping and even jousting – a sport that is particularly popular in Uzbekistan. One entertaining event that originated in Russia and which is pursued at Izmailova Park is pushball. Two teams attempt to push a huge soft ball over their opponents' goal line. This requires a bold pony: one who is quite prepared to lend its weight and is trained to do most of the pushing. Once the ball starts rolling, it is extremely difficult to stop it except by lining up the defence in its path. The arenas where these various competitions take place are unusually elegant and the crowds who flock to them in large numbers are colourful and excited.

As a result of this emphasis on competition, much has been done to select the right kind of horse for training and for the different departments of sport. Great emphasis is put on matching horse and rider. This relationship is considered of paramount importance. In the early days when the schools were using only rejects, it was impossible to achieve this; now all schools are able to use Thoroughbreds, selected for their suitability, training and performance.

It is interesting that James Fillis, an Englishman who became chief *écuyer* in St Petersburg, had such a profound influence on Russian equitation. He once stated, 'I prefer Thoroughbreds; whoever has ridden a Thoroughbred will never ride anything else.' The Russians have taken this advice very much to heart, but Burevestnik has had to devote a great deal of thought to selecting its horses because there are

ABOVE *The emphasis on competition work has encouraged selective breeding to produce a type suitable for the demands of competitive riding in Russia. A Thoroughbred stallion raised on the Tori State Farm in Estonia.*

many breeds and types, some of which are more suitable for certain kinds of riding than others. At Burevestnik, however, there does seem to be a very definite type of horse used; medium-sized – you seldom see a Russian horse over sixteen hands – strong and able to stand up to the pressures of competitive Russian riding and, of course, the terrain. Ivanov himself prefers horses who have had some experience in racing, as he finds them more adaptable; they need not necessarily have had a good track record, but their experience on the track generally proves, he believes, to be of value in their later training. The horses, of course, are all owned by the state farms or studs, which have to be persuaded to send them to Burevestnik if they are thought to be particularly suitable. When a good horse has been found, it is then necessary to find a suitable rider.

Ivanov is very much a traditionalist – in both the style of riding and the purpose to which he feels the riding of horses should be put. He likes

OPPOSITE *The famous Orlov trotter. Count Orlov-Chesmenki founded the breed in the eighteenth century with his stallion Bars I (above). The Orlov today; Kvadrat, a champion stallion at the First Moscow Stud (below).*

to talk of his 'Moscow School of Vienna' and not surprisingly dressage and *haute école* play an important part in his school; but, as at Vienna, he goes even further, believing in the performance of carousels and eighteenth-century movements illustrating the ability of a horse to perform difficult movements when properly trained and ridden. Every action or movement of both horse and rider must have beauty of style as its aim.

The history of the Russian successes in the international field is somewhat chequered. It was not until 1958 that the Russians first appeared from behind the Iron Curtain, paying a surprise visit to Aachen. Their first major success in show jumping coincided with their first visit to Paris, when they won the Nations Cup. In 1973 they were second in the European three-day-event championship at Kiev – a competition they had previously won at the Burghley Horse Trials in 1965, coming second in 1971. Emphasis is still very much on success, but one cannot help feeling that it would be more easily come by if Russians were able to perform more frequently in other European countries.

Although those taking part in competitions come mostly from the schools and clubs such as Burevestnik, riding lessons are now available at collective and stud farms for other riders. There are some seventy state stud farms which breed riding, racing and draught horses, as well as trotters, which provide what is probably the most popular equestrian sport in Russia.

It is fitting that Izmailova Park should be the centre of all this equestrian activity. Only fifty years ago it was a small suburb of Moscow; there still stood on the banks of the Ismailova River (known now as the Serebrianka) the abandoned seventeenth-century palace and the majestic Pokrovsky Cathedral, with its five cupolas, built by master stonemasons and decorated with brilliantly coloured tiles. Now there are a quarter of a million inhabitants in this district, with large residential centres, cinemas, restaurants and shops and, in addition to the Burevestnik Society, there is a large sports and recreational complex run by the State Central Order of Lenin. The park itself, immense and picturesque, is an excellent retreat from the noise of the city. It can be compared with any of the finest parks in the European capitals; in fact, it is ten times the size of Hyde Park and five times that of Central Park in New York.

OPPOSITE *Two very different Russian native breeds. Don trotting horses; a well-proportioned, hardy breed, the Don horse is an equally good saddle or light-draught horse* (above). *The Russian heavy-draught horse, standing about sixteen hands with a wide back and deep girth, is ideal for work on the land* (below).

In the 1660s Tsar Alexis Mikhailovich instituted a large agricultural complex with orchards and game reserves at Izmailova. The origin of the park's name has been much discussed. It has remained unchanged for centuries and it is thought to refer to the Russian phrase 'exhausted by life'. Alternatively it could be translated as 'languished', derived from the story of a famous hunter who fell into a quagmire and languished until he was rescued.

Tsar Alexis's project was the first attempt at modern farming in Russia. It was, by early standards, a sophisticated economic venture. A thousand serfs were employed, new farming techniques were adopted, and, within a very short space of time, a successful and prosperous business was established. The greatest impact of Alexis's experiment was the freedom it granted Moscow from its former dependence on foreign imports. It was an example to be followed by other great landowners. The Tsar built mills and processed cereals. He set up a dairy, glasshouse and foundry. A linen industry flourished. He also produced wine. He stocked the land with a wide and remarkable variety of animals – elk, wolves, foxes, tigers, lions, panthers and an elephant presented by the Shah of Persia. Over fifty thousand horses were kept at Izmailova – these being in constant demand for travelling, lavish retinues and processions, not to mention the cavalry, hunting and farming.

On his death in 1676 the estate passed to Tsar Feodor Alexeev who had neither the skill nor the interest of his father. The estate then became the residence of the regent, Princess Sophia. During this period of Court intrigue and murder, Izmailova became the childhood retreat for Peter the Great, another innovator. Thus Izmailova came into its own once again. With his passion for war games, Peter turned the park into a training ground. He played at soldiers, drilling his playmates into regiments with the deadly seriousness of a brilliant child. Real weapons were used in their mock battles, and fortifications were built, the remains of which can still be seen. At the cost of many wounds and a few deaths, the 'play soldiers' began to turn into real regiments, one of which was to be named after Izmailova.

After Peter's death the park became a place for recreation and hunting; there were no less than one thousand different kinds of animals in the grounds in the middle of the nineteenth century. Hunting was not just a hobby, for food and clothing were acquired from the animals.

OPPOSITE *A troika demonstration at the First Moscow Stud. In racing, the middle horse between the shafts moves at the trot while the outside horses, hitched to the carriage, are moving at the gallop* (above). *A horse-drawn skiing competition on the snow-covered Hippodrome circuit* (below).

ABOVE *A jumping competition in the Burevestnik school.* OPPOSITE *The Russians have established themselves as a team to be reckoned with in eventing. The European Championships were held in Kiev in 1973. Two of Russia's international three-day-event riders in action; Saboital Mursalimov* (above) *and Pavel Deyev* (below).

Some of the top international riders in Russia. Ivan Kalita on his favourite horse, Absinthe (left). Tatiana Kulikovskaya, a former USSR champion (below). Elena Petushkova, world dressage champion (right). Sergei Filatov, an Olympic gold medal winner (far right).

Laws concerning interference with them, their breeding and development were very strict, any infringement being severely punished. The park fell into disrepair at the time of Catherine II and, in 1812, the estate was ravaged by the French troops. Under Nicholas I it became a rest home for aged soldiers from the Izmailova regiment – the regiment originally established by Peter the Great. At the beginning of this century it once again became an area of experimentation; some distance from the centre of the city, it seemed an ideal place to hold meetings and it was at Izmailova that the revolutionaries of the early years of the twentieth century met in secrecy and safety.

Izmailova is a setting with a wonderfully romantic background, fitting, indeed, for equestrianism in Russia which has had to survive such great difficulties; but which, thanks to the Burevestnik Club and others of a similar nature, is making great strides forward, as is shown by the success of their riders in competition, particularly in dressage and cross-country riding.

Club de Campo and
Club Deportivo Las Lomas, Madrid

Spain

At the conference held for Fédération Equestre Internationale instructors at the National Equestrian Centre, Stoneleigh in April 1971 a member of the Spanish federation, Colonel Ybarro, noted that although there is an increasing interest in riding in Spain – especially among the young – there is a shortage of trained civilian instructors. Until recently riding has been the preserve of the military and the very wealthy. Civilian instructors were invariably retired cavalry officers and the main centre for instruction was the Centre Sportive Militaire. Spain still has an active cavalry, as large as any in Europe, and like most other countries a tradition of equestrianism has depended on it. But with the growing demands from the civilian sector the military can no longer be relied on to provide sufficient numbers of qualified instructors.

Private enterprise has moved in to fill the gap: to accommodate the ever increasing enthusiasm for riding instruction and facilities, and to produce a body of civilian riders from which the instructors of the future can be drawn. There is no doubt that the most progressive riding in Spain is now to be found in the many clubs emerging in the major cities. The outstanding club is the Sociedad Hipica Española Club de Campo situated close to the centre of Madrid. One is constantly amazed that a site of such magnitude – one thousand acres – can be part of a European capital of over three-and-a-half million people. Originally on the outskirts of the city, it has now been surrounded by the expanding metropolis. The grandson of one of the founders of the club, Count Alfonso de Aliaga, who lives in the magnificent palace in Princessa Street in the very heart of Madrid, has his horses ridden from the palace stables to the Club de Campo every morning to be exercised. The ride takes just twenty minutes.

Although the club was opened in 1918 the white buildings with tiled roofs, gardens and grounds have a timeless quality – enhanced by their isolation from the bustle of the city so close at hand. It is not surprising that the club is popular enough to attract more than 32,000 members each of whom is prepared to pay as much as £2,000 ($5,000) to join, and then to pay an annual subscription of £5 or £6 ($15). Their membership entitles them to the use of the golf course and tennis courts and innumerable other facilities; also to avail themselves of the restaurant and bar. But this is all in addition to the magnificent equestrian

PREVIOUS PAGES *The Sociedad Hipica Española Club de Campo. As well as the show ground, gallops, dressage arenas, polo ground, cross-country course and indoor school, there are other sporting facilities such as a golf course and tennis courts.*

amenities: the famous show ground, the many rings, dressage arenas, gallops, polo ground, cross-country course and indoor school.

There are no less than 308 stables at the club and between 250 and 300 horses are permanently stabled there. The majority of these belong to members who keep them there at livery, riding them in the early morning, evenings and at weekends. There are a limited number of horses owned by the club which are kept for hiring out. Forty-five grooms are fully employed, each being responsible for up to eight horses. In addition there is a ground staff of over sixty. This figure, though seemingly excessive, is not surprising when one sees how well-kept the whole complex is. Instruction is in the hands of three full-time instructors who are involved for the most part with beginners. More experienced riders, especially those of national and international calibre, have their own trainers, either for show-jumping or dressage. The senior international team trainer in residence is at present Señor Manero.

The stables, attached to the entrance of the club and therefore the first part one sees, are laid out in series of blocks – each with fifteen or sixteen looseboxes, the average size of each being ten feet by ten feet. Some are a little smaller and all have a stone manger built into the wall. Solid and streamlined, they are painted in blue and white. In each case the block forms three sides of a square with a beautifully designed courtyard, and at each end there are tack rooms, saddle rooms and cleaning areas. Immediately facing the stables, and easily accessible, are small lungeing rings and loose schools where horses can be put over fences without a rider or without a lunge.

The *pièce de résistance* of the whole complex is the splendid indoor school. It was completed in 1968 and opened by Generalissimo Franco himself in the presence of Don José Luis Rivas the Minister of Sport and of course the director of the club, Don Carlos Kirkpatrick O'Donnell. In the foyer one is greeted by a handsome Dalby while in the bar there is a fine sporting painting by W. Shayer. The school itself is seventy by thirty-five metres, with a cement roof built on the cantilever principle providing a wide span free of supports. The floor is of light sand and although there is plenty of space for spectators there are no formal seats, merely concrete tiers. Probably any number between six hundred and a thousand can watch what is going on in the school from these tiered platforms. The sides are of corrugated iron and there are sliding windows.

I understand that when more money is available the cement and iron will be covered by some additional material.

Beyond the stables, the indoor school and the lunge rings, is the very fine and justifiably famous show ground which can only be described as a miniature Ballsbridge, Dublin. It is surrounded by a box hedge and white railings with excellent stands, at the back of which are private boxes, a presidential box and a well located box for judges and jury. The ring is extremely picturesque. Flanked by trees, it is reminiscent of the Piazza de Sienna, Rome; neither wholly circular nor quite rectangular in shape with a permanent water jump. The show ground is only used once a year for the Spanish International Show because due to the limited amount of rain in this part of the world the grass dries up very quickly. The show ground is probably unique in being completely green for only one week of each year.

Behind the show ground there is a circle of covered stalls where the horses taking part in the competitions are temporarily stabled during the day, using the club stables at night. There is an adequate 'pocket' which is approached from a very large collecting ring with a large number of practice jumps. In addition there are two practice rings, considerably larger than the show arena itself. In one there are no less than thirty fences, including banks, ditches and so on – all permanently available for the members of the club to practise over. There are also two full-sized dressage arenas which can be used at all times of the day and in all weather despite the fact that the sand would seem to be on the heavy side – especially in damp weather. The ground staff is responsible for keeping all these arenas in immaculate condition, properly raked, rolled and harrowed.

Adjacent to the second practice arena which is 150 by 100 metres, there is a small show-jumping arena designed specially to enable people to practise in a limited area if they are planning to attend a show ground where the arena is likely to be small. There is also an exercising ground which is even larger than the practice arenas. Completely surrounding this extensive area of rings and arenas is a sand track no less than 1,500 metres long which is used as a gallop. Outside this is yet

OPPOSITE *The* pièce de résistance *of the Club de Campo is the splendid indoor school, completed in 1968. The cantilevered cement roof provides a wide span free of supports, and the concrete tiers can accommodate up to a thousand spectators* (above). *The famous show ground is used only once a year, for the Spanish International Show* (centre). *Flanked by trees, the ground has excellent stands, a presidential box and a well-sited judges' box* (below).

another track – a gallop with fences at regular intervals. All round and between the tracks are shrubs, trees and flowers.

There is always something going on at this impressive centre, but it is on Sundays that the club really becomes a hive of activity. Competitions are held between clubs of a similar nature in show jumping and dressage while other members make use of the golf course, tennis courts and pigeon shooting – not to mention the other sporting facilities available. A particularly valuable amenity is the special children's playground where youngsters can be happily occupied while their parents are taking part in one of the sports or patronising the bars and restaurant. Surprisingly few children, however, are actually seen riding at the club. This is true all over Spain although this is gradually changing. The problem is very similar to that found in Italy: there are very few ponies and the tendency is for a child to start riding considerably later than in countries where ponies are an accepted part of the equestrian scene.

With such facilities at the Club de Campo and the many other clubs, the standard of riding is improving all the time. Correspondingly, the performance of Spanish riders in the international field is also very high, especially under the team trainer Señor Manero. Leading international riders in Spain include the show jumpers Segovia, Alvarez, Vallejo Goyago de Llano. The main enthusiasm is for show jumping. In dressage and three-day eventing the Spanish do not, at present, consider themselves up to Olympic standards, though it is interesting to note that the intrepid Duque de Albuquerque, a gallant rider on many occasions in the English Grand National, was in the Spanish three-day-event team in the Rome Olympics of 1960.

Typical of a rather different type of club, but very similar to many others in Spain, is the Club Deportivo Las Lomas. Opened only last March by Generalissimo Franco, it is situated some ten or twelve miles from Madrid in fine open country. The fact that Franco opened both the Club de Campo and Las Lomas is indicative of the official interest shown in equestrian affairs.

At this club, which is part of a big development complex, there are about a thousand members, the majority of whom are shareholders in the development company. This scheme is very similar to those being developed in other parts of the world, notably in America where the

OPPOSITE *The stable area at the Club Deportivo Las Lomas. Some seventy horses are stabled in these thatch-roofed looseboxes.*

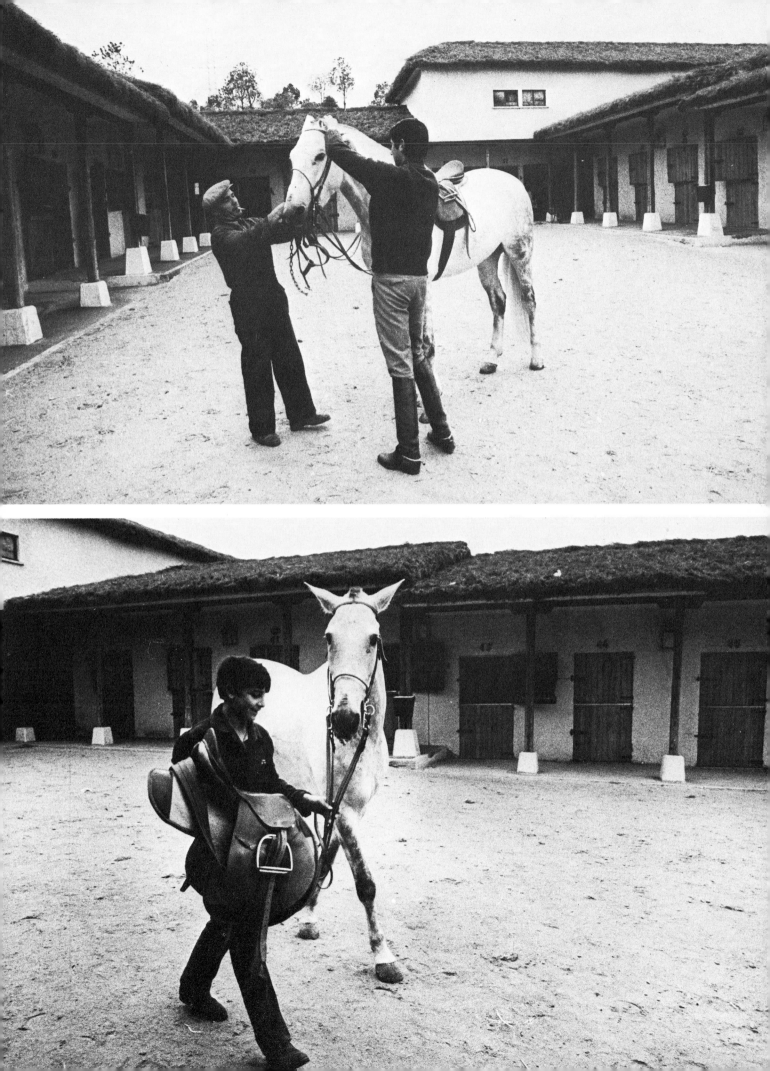

best known is Diamond Bar outside Los Angeles, and the one in the Algarve region of Portugal at Vilamoura, the openings of both of which I was privileged to attend.

There is a small annual subscription at Las Lomas and there is no doubt that members get full value for money. Some seventy horses are stabled in elegant, if slightly small stables with thatched roofs. Built in blocks, each with about twenty looseboxes, all is on a more modest scale than at the Club de Campo although plans for expansion are being discussed. As with the Club de Campo a limited number of horses can be hired, but the majority belong to the club members who can ride anywhere in the area where, in addition, a cross-country course is being built.

Not unlike the Club de Campo the emphasis has been for a long time on show jumping, but the spectrum of events is widening. The senior instructor and director of the club, Señor Antonio Alvarez Acedo, has been instrumental in arranging competitions both on a social and national level. These are held regularly and have been a great success – so much so in fact that Las Lomas has been chosen to hold the junior show jumping championships of Spain in 1974. In addition to Señor Antonio Alvarez Acedo there are four full-time instructors and nine grooms – three at each level: three senior grooms, three learner grooms and three students.

There is a small but adequate and well-designed club house with changing rooms and, upstairs, a bar and lounge. The lounge is noteworthy for two paintings by Herring from the Fores National Sports Series, one of which is particularly interesting. It clearly shows the development of the top boot as it is known today. One of the riders has the boot well up over the knee and up the thigh, as was originally worn to protect the trousers from mud, but when jumping came in and the length of leathers had to be shortened, it was found that the boot behind the knee was uncomfortable: the top was therefore turned over, as can clearly be seen in the boots of another rider, having the tan-coloured top, which only reached the knee.

OPPOSITE *Antonio Alvarez Acedo, the director and senior instructor of the club, performs the Spanish Walk* (above). *The director's youngest son practises in the indoor school. Sixty-five by twenty-five metres, it has a long gallery down one side and an unusual glass wall on the other* (below).

The centrepiece of Las Lomas is undoubtedly the very fine indoor school. It is sixty-five by twenty-five metres with a long gallery at one side. On the opposite side a glass wall is so designed that one can see out but people from the outside cannot see in. Particularly striking is the glass window mosaic at one end of the school with an equestrian design. At the other end is a jump store, in the centre is a jury box and the president's box, and high pine kicking boards surround the school. The school is only a few yards from the stable area, which is on a bank and which, in addition to the looseboxes, has a very practical saddle room where no less than sixty saddles are housed, some twenty of them all round a centre pillar, which is extremely cleverly designed.

As at de Campo there is a loose ring, but the outside rings of Las Lomas are constructed on the American estancia style with large, light poles. Interesting is the use of rails made of plastic. In the spacious, open show jumping arena, seventy-five metres by one hundred metres, the rails round the outside are stronger, being made of iron and painted white. There is a 600-metre gallop around the perimeter, going round the back of a stand which runs down one side of the show jumping arena and which can seat about five hundred people. There is also a beginners' arena, twenty by thirty metres, and small arenas for schooling on the ground.

Although Las Lomas is far less ambitious than the Club de Campo, there can be no doubt that it serves an extremely useful purpose and is well supported: perhaps by a rather different section of society to that which supplies the members of de Campo. All these clubs are self-supporting for there is no government help although interest and encouragement from the state is shown in many ways.

These clubs are still very dependent upon the military for their instructors, and as there is fortunately still a cavalry in Spain the standard of instruction remains high. There is little doubt that there is a general overall improvement in riding standards and also it is evident the number of people wishing to ride is increasing as standards of living improve.

Spain should, indeed, consider itself fortunate that private enterprise has been prepared to invest in such a large way in the sport and

OPPOSITE *Although the spectrum of events is widening, the emphasis at Las Lomas has long been on show jumping. Competitions at both social and national levels are held regularly. Around the outdoor arena there is a 600-metre gallop.*

recreation of riding. There is no country in the world that would not envy the superb lay-out of the Club de Campo or the magnificent setting of Las Lomas. Spain is fully aware of the need to provide more civilian instructors to take the place of the cavalry instructors, but with such amenities it seems likely that the number of civilian instructors available will increase every year. It would seem likely that in the course of time there will come into being a national centre: or more likely perhaps, one of the existing clubs will attain national status. Certainly both clubs described here would be justified in being so titled.

ABOVE *With the increasing enthusiasm for riding in Spain – particularly among the young – the riding clubs have a vital part to play in supplying instructors of the future.*
OPPOSITE *The Club Deportivo Las Lomas: the centrepiece of the school, the indoor* manège *with its glass mosaic and spacious arena.* OVERLEAF *An inspection before morning exercise in the stable yard at Las Lomas.*

Centro Ippico di Castellazzo, Milan

OPPOSITE *Centro Ippico di Castellazzo: morning training for Graziano Mancinelli* (above) *; one of the two indoor schools available for club members* (below).

Italy

Because of the great national and international reputation of Caprilli, Italy will always have a considerable reputation in the equestrian world, although by today's standards there is possibly less attention paid to riding in Italy than in most European countries; nor is it wholly untrue to say that for Italians riding is still an exclusive recreation. Italy has yet to experience the awakening of popular interest such as has occurred in England and Germany.

In Italy there are two completely separate centres of equestrianism: Rome and Milan. As far as Rome is concerned, there are the famous d'Inzeo brothers and the only important hunt in Italy – the Rome Foxhounds. But Milan, in the industrial north, is the centre of more intensive riding activity. There are about half a dozen successful riding schools in or near Milan – most of them lavishly financed by wealthy industrialists; but without any doubt the most outstanding of these is the internationally renowned school connected with Graziano Mancinelli, the Italian show jumper and winner of the individual gold medal at Munich in 1972. The Centro Ippico di Castellazzo – The Castle Riding Centre – is just outside Milan. More a club than a school, it is owned by Donna Beatrice Binelli Crivelli. Her home, the Castellazzo Villa, is a beautiful mellow-walled house, and Donna Beatrice herself seems more the patron of the school rather than the president, though the latter is her official title. The school is situated on the estate of her family, and her mother, Giustina Crivelli di Agliate, who could be described as the lady of the manor, was the first president.

Although it is a modern building, the club, only half a mile from the Castellazzo Villa, has considerable attraction. With a concrete and timber façade and flowering and climbing plants creeping up the walls, it blends in well. The centrepiece is the larger of the two indoor schools, with a gallery, bar and restaurant and, at ground level, linking corridors to the stables which are constructed of red brick.

The club consists of two hundred members who have the use of the two indoor schools – the main one of thirty by sixty metres, the other forty by twenty metres. During the winter an additional school is made available by means of a large inflated tent. An outdoor area with a sand surface and a good supply of conventional and easily portable fences is also

OPPOSITE *The club house at the Centro Ippico di Castellazzo, just outside Milan, the most celebrated of the half dozen riding schools in the area* (above). *There are two main indoor schools at Castellazzo, one thirty by sixty metres and the other forty by twenty metres. During the winter a large inflatable tent serves as an additional indoor school* (below).

Italy

The club has two hundred members and places special emphasis on the instruction of young riders.

maintained. There is a cross-country course with what are regarded as the standard obstacles – coffin, banks, timber and brush fences – but this is now in a state of neglect. Knee-high in grass it is seldom used these days although it was incorporated in part of the Italian Jumping Derby which took place at the centre in 1969.

There are no less than eighty-six looseboxes, filled practically all the time though only five horses belong to the club; the remainder belong to members who pay some £70 ($175) per month for livery and the use of the various facilities – among which is a blacksmith's forge with a blacksmith in permanent attendance. In addition, members pay an annual subscription of £100 ($250). Not surprisingly the school is financially independent and inclined to be exclusive.

The modern complex is complemented and supported by excellent staff. The club has a full-time managing director, Dr Gian Franco Boveri, who speaks fluent English and has an enviable breadth of outlook. There is also a full-time chief instructor, Giuliano Fantarelli. Close to thirty grooms cater to the needs of the members. Such a large number of horses is difficult to maintain as good grooms are, apparently, becoming increasingly difficult to get, although with plenty of cheap labour available from the south it is probably easier to staff stables in Milan than in most parts of the world. Certainly the riding schools, racing stables and studs are remarkably well-kept and unusually well-staffed.

A feature of this club is the interest taken in the younger pupils, for whom there is a special instructor, Mario Tome. Although there is this emphasis on young riders, there are no ponies at the school. Children are expected to learn to ride on horses – Thoroughbreds or Arabs – and as a result, they cannot really start until they are in their early teens. Once they do begin to ride, these juniors have before them an exceptional model, Graziano Mancinelli. Understandably, as Mancinelli is so closely connected with the school, the pupils tend to adopt his style of riding, but Mancinelli himself does not teach in the formal sense of the word; rather he works there constantly, spending a great deal of time schooling, especially in the winter months when he is making young horses.

Over the years there has been considerable controversy about the status of Mancinelli as a rider. There is little doubt that in his early days he did have employment, if not as an instructor at least as a breaker and trainer of young horses. In the opinion of many, therefore, he should be

OVERLEAF *The red-brick stables at Castellazzo; nearly all the horses in the eighty-six looseboxes belong to the members, who pay about £70 ($175) a month for livery.*

classified as a professional rider, which would of course debar him from the Olympic Games. But this is really a futile argument as the Olympic Committee has accepted him as an amateur and indeed he has ridden in four Olympics, winning a gold medal at the Munich Games.

Mancinelli's regular appearances at the club give the younger members ample opportunity to observe and in many instances copy him. The views of the chief instructor Fantarelli on this subject are not without interest. He admits that too many of the pupils try to imitate Mancinelli and he says, what works for Mancinelli does not necessarily work for everyone else. The principal, Dr Boveri, says: 'The main influence at this school is, without any possible doubt, Graziano Mancinelli. His character, his sensitivity with the horse – when he rides he is one with his horse – is extremely impressive. In addition, he is very keen on studying the character of a horse and assessing its potential; and, indeed, he is able to obtain the absolute maximum possible from any horse that he rides. His training is patient and, therefore, slow.'

It seems that Mancinelli does take a lot of trouble when advising others in finding the right horse for the right rider, so that they can train together – a principle that he follows himself. This was a tradition that was emphasised by the great Caprilli here at Milan. Obviously today things are more flexible; it is not easy to adhere precisely to Caprilli's old system but, as in his day, a great deal of work is done on the ground before a horse or rider is allowed to jump.

'Although the Derby course was built here [Dr Boveri says], we do not train very much over permanent fences. We believe that it takes at least four or five years to bring one of our pupils – and he has to be a promising pupil – up to international show jumping standard. In our club (and here wc are reflecting the mind of Mancinelli himself and our senior instructors) we follow the precept that the horse is never wrong; it is always the rider that is wrong. No one here is ever allowed to thrash a horse, or to be cruel in any other way.'

Mancinelli came up from Rome when he was only sixteen and he first started riding at a very small club which was closely associated with Castellazzo in earlier times. As Mancinelli grew up, the interest in riding in Italy was becoming more widespread. Show jumping clubs are now mushrooming, but like most countries in Europe – indeed, the whole world – Italy is short of top-class instructors. The National Federation

The club, like most equestrian establishments in Italy, is unusually well-staffed and has a high standard of stable management.

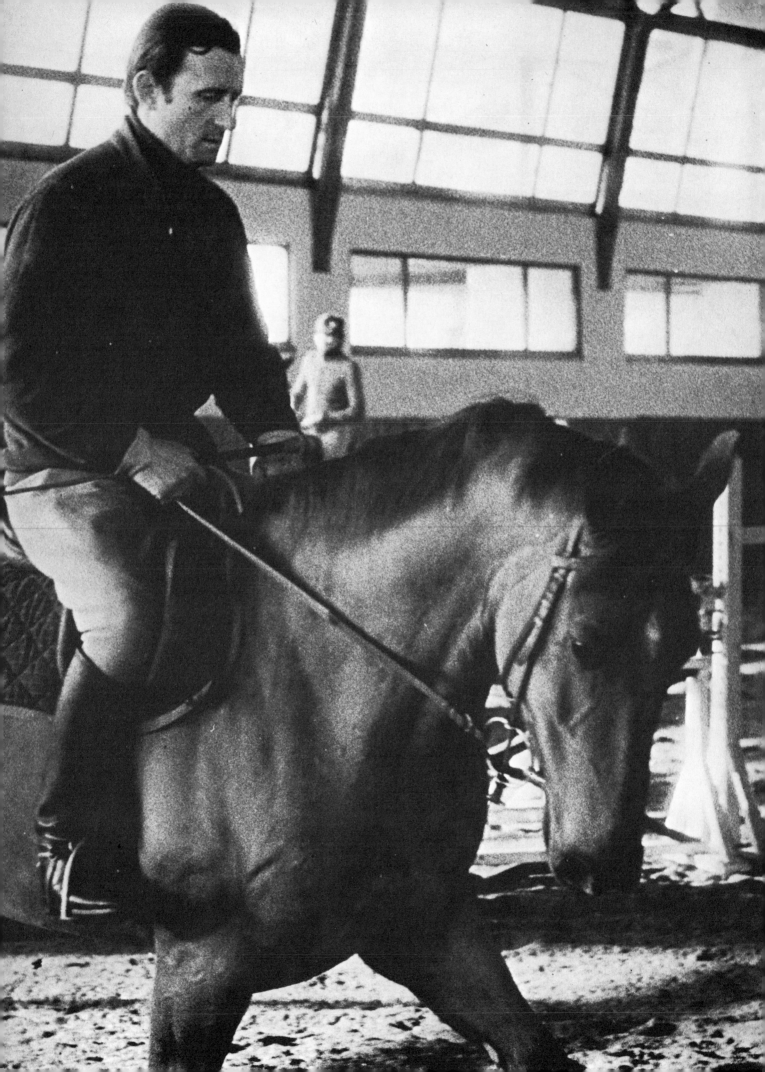

attempted to start a really good training school in Rome. Unfortunately the school had to be closed, though whether it was through lack of money or lack of support is not wholly clear.

There is no doubt that the chief instructor Fantarelli has learned a great deal from Mancinelli and thus there is a chain of teaching in the club. Unfortunately, there are neither instructors' exams nor any form of licensing of instructors in Italy. As with most countries, at least until recently, riding in Italy has depended on the old instructors from the cavalry regiments, and until 1940, these were of a high standard. Today very few army officers in Italy ride and there is, surprisingly and sadly, no military school of riding.

Despite the world-wide reputation of the d'Inzeos and Mancinelli, and the lustre that their names have brought to Italy, the government gives only meagre support to equestrianism and such support as it does give consists almost entirely of prize money at international shows, additional prize money always being given to winners on Italian-bred horses. Consequently over the last year or two there has been a definite

OPPOSITE AND ABOVE *The name of Graziano Mancinelli, international show jumper and Olympic gold-medallist, is closely associated with the Castellazzo. Although he does no formal teaching, his influence on the pupils' riding style is considerable.*

Italy

swing from Irish-bred to Italian-bred horses. There is a drawback to this policy however. Although there has been an upsurge of riding in Italy since the War, especially in the north, the emphasis has been different to any other European country. There is virtually no hunting, and riding for riding's sake does not seem to satisfy the average Italian horseman. It is, therefore, show jumping that is the main equestrian interest and it is quite obvious that Italians like not only to compete but to win. It is not an unfair comment to say that the Italians are more interested in competing on horses than in horses themselves. Riding outside, if not completely unknown, is practised very little. It is show jumping, and invariably show jumping indoors, that appeals to the Italian horseman.

Even Mancinelli seldom lets a horse down, let alone turns it out to grass; they are used the full year round. It should, however, be pointed out that many great Continental experts have considered the British passion for turning horses out to grass in the summer a typical English madness. 'You take four months', they say, 'to get a horse fit and then, as soon as it is in shape you turn it out to grass and so it loses all its fitness.' Obviously there are two points of view here, and there is no doubt whatever to which point of view the Italians subscribe.

Riding in Italy continues to be conducted on a club basis and there is no doubt that business is booming in the Italian equestrian world. Endless new clubs are coming into being with excellent facilities. Perhaps because Italy has always been in the fore in architectural planning, the schools are frequently very fine to look at. Around Milan, the design centre of Italy, the means for attractive modern air-conditioned schools have been found. Comfort and convenience are not treated lightly. Amenities usually include showers, changing rooms, bars and restaurants; even terraces with umbrella-shaded tables overlooking a working area or showground. It would seem that such additions are very much a priority in Italy.

The traditional rivalry between the north and the south – Milan and Rome – still exists and is reflected in the horse world, as in so many other aspects of Italian life. Milanese show jumpers concede that the d'Inzeos have made a major contribution, but that is where it ends as far as Rome is concerned. They refer, with a certain pleasure, to the collapse of the proposed national school in Rome. This division may have hampered

OPPOSITE *Mancinelli and The Rock, that famous grey with whom Piero d'Inzeo had such success, competing for the Horse and Hound Cup at the Royal International Horse Show, London, in 1963.*

Italy

Italy's development. Certainly from a distance it seems strange that Italian riders have not relied more on the great Italian cavalry traditions, but have preferred to start afresh. One of the results of this is a certain lack of unity and an increased dependence on individual talent; hence the status of Mancinelli in the north and the status, no less, of the d'Inzeos in the south, but they might have come from different planets.

In his book *More Than Victory Alone* Piero d'Inzeo has this to say: 'The Italian school, guardian of the first doctrine, started off well but was left almost at the start because it did not take the trouble to delve into the problems of willpower and self-denial. Basically the Italians have made tragically little use of Caprilli's principles, whereas other countries have used them to far greater advantage.' Certainly there has been no concerted effort to analyse the achievements of the past but, nevertheless, one gets the impression that the Italians have, unconsciously perhaps, made more use of Caprilli's principles than d'Inzeo suggests.

Rome was not in the forefront of riding in the early days, but it developed steadily and effectively until at the time of Pliny most of the more spacious villas had hippodromes which could be used – and, indeed, were used – for riding. In the Middle Ages Italians were the most advanced as far as breeding and racing were concerned. It is in no way surprising, therefore, that it was Italy which eventually produced the great Caprilli – generally regarded as the inventor of the forward seat. It is difficult, perhaps, to appreciate that Caprilli was only of the twentieth century, so entirely accepted are his principles today. His secret was simple, though it took some time to discover it; to observe and study the way a horse moved at every gait, above all when jumping, and then to consider the way in which he could be supported and spared any suffering or undue effort while remaining under the control of the rider. Caprilli envisaged a rider who would follow with his horse, accompanying him as one in his movements and seconding him completely with his arms and body, while keeping his knees always firm and his legs as they fell naturally, riding solidly on the fork. He realised the necessity of bringing down the crutch into the saddle, which led to the heels-down style, the sole of the foot turned slightly out as a means of imparting firmness to the lower part of the body. The difference between natural equitation and what is sometimes known as 'school' equitation lies in the fact that, while the latter strives to adapt the horse to the horseman, the former, in contrast, is designed to fit the horseman to the horse.

Caprilli, unfortunately, left comparatively little in writing for students to follow, but the results achieved by his pupils were so remarkable that every serious horseman in Europe, especially those whose function it was to instruct, particularly in the art of jumping, have appreciated the enormous advance he made in the theory of equitation. Today Caprilli is a household word in the world of the horse and it is not surprising that, consciously or unconsciously, the Italian riders have shown their indebtedness to him.

Exactly how much they – and indeed all riders – owe to Caprilli is perhaps best revealed in his own words:

'With the understanding that balance and firmness in the saddle are the *sine qua non*, let us now look at what, in my opinion, is required of a rider in the jump: to accompany with the weight of his body – with the hands, especially – every movement the horse makes, offering him no interference. Furthermore, and more particularly, as the horse approaches the obstacle the rider should permit him to stretch his neck and head forward, and the rider should move his hands up so that the animal can do so without losing contact or slackening on the reins, but maintaining a constant light tension.

'Next, when the horse draws back his head and neck and shifts his centre of gravity back, putting the weight on the haunches, the rider should bring his hands back a bit, taking care not to increase tension on the reins too much.

'Just as soon as the horse has sprung, the rider should let his trunk follow the displacement forward of the centre of gravity without, however, lifting his seat too far out of the saddle. At the very same instant he should allow the horse to stretch his neck and shoulders, which is an extremely important movement, and essential to the horse's completing the jump without being hurt, by moving his hands forward as far as possible, and giving the horse full rein, letting the reins slip through his fingers should that be necessary.

'You will see that this "following" when the horse is in the air is of prime importance. The slightest bother the rider causes the horse at this moment will not only prejudice the jump but inflict pain that will go from his mouth to his loins and might even, as often happens, make him hit the obstacle with his hind legs.

Centro Ippico di Castellazzo, Milan

'If the rider does not yield when he is in the air, and does not follow
the horse's shift in weight by moving his trunk, the animal will be dis-
heartened, and innumerable difficulties are bound to arise out of his
attitude. Furthermore, he will learn to land foursquare, which is very
hard on the loins and calls for greater effort from the horse than does
hitting the ground correctly. The rider's shifting his upper body forward,
therefore, should be slight, but sufficient to permit him to be ready to take
control of the horse should the animal hit the obstacle or stumble when
he hits the ground.

'In conclusion, I believe that following by the rider when the horse is
off the ground is the most important action of all on his part, and it is
therefore the movement the instructor should insist upon and see that
every rider achieves.

'Aiding the horse systematically, a thing many would like to see during
the jump, is something that cannot be done at times; and in some instances, in my view, it has bad consequences. It often happens that the
horse, fearing the aid, rushes during the last part of his approach to the
obstacle and seriously compromises the jump.

'A good jumper does not have to be aided in his jump, for once he has
gauged the obstacle he knows just how much force he needs to get over
it without the rider demanding it of him superfluously. Mediocre and
inexpert jumpers can become good ones through rational and continuous
practice, but never through the employment of aids or violent means.

'Occasionally, in exceptional cases, aid may be useful in the last two
or three beats of the gallop and at the moment when the horse is just
about to take off, if he shows signs of holding back by hesitating. One
must, however, always be cautious in giving aid, and do so in the
appropriate measure. You must cease any aid the moment the horse
indicates that all is well. At all cost, avoid moving the hands out to the
sides, instead, move them up, easing up on the reins. Remember that
moving the hands is extremely harmful, since this keeps the horse from
being able to observe where he is going, and therefore gives him an
excuse to balk or to be off in his timing.

'Never put a timid or fearful horse over a high obstacle. Such horses
should practice with low obstacles, preferably at a slow gait, and be given
the opportunity to see the obstacle clearly, even smelling it if necessary.
Do your best to discover just what it is that frightens the horse or makes

OPPOSITE *The traditional rivalry between north and south – Milan and Rome – is personified in*
Mancinelli and the d'Inzeo brothers. Piero d'Inzeo riding Ballyblak in the Prince of Wales Cup at the 1965
Royal International Horse Show.

169

him timid, and try to eliminate that factor. When that has been done, but not before, you can begin gradually to increase the height of the obstacle. With nervous horses, the rider should even avoid squeezing them at the fork or alarming them by taking them up too much, for this will make them bolt or confuse them.

'I have limited myself in this study to outlining a few basic principles, and have certainly left many lacunae, but the principle that I have sought to place in evidence and what, as I see it, is the fundamental rule for all equitation in the field, is always to second and favour the horse's natural instincts and attitudes, and avoid giving him any undue pain while working. With rigorous application of that principle, which comes through the simple employment of a few uncomplicated rules, the horse, submissive by nature, will not regress, but will display the many gifts that have made him a precious instrument of warfare throughout the ages.

'I close, then, with the fervid hope that these few thoughts, fruit of experience by no means brief – that have received even the approval of many foreign officers with whom I have had occasion to exchange ideas – will receive the dissemination and approbation throughout our cavalry that they seem to me to merit and that they become touchstones of military equitation to pass on to the men.'

Mancinelli, of course, is an exaggeration of all this. His style can hardly be described as that found in the manual; it is tremendously enthusiastic and exciting – inspired even. In his own way he is a perfectionist, though to the classicist his style is extravagant and certainly not one to be copied, though, as has been suggested above, many riders are in fact attempting to do so. Particularly interesting are his hands, whose action is completely independent of the shoulders and the rest of his body. His wrists seem extraordinarily supple, so that, although there is great activity in his body when jumping, he nevertheless seldom interferes with his horse's mouth. Mancinelli has been known to say that when he works, his leg is where it belongs, but when he is competing, that is another matter altogether. He even goes further and insists that when competing you have to keep moving at all costs and that, he says, you cannot do it stylishly. On today's courses style leads to refusals and you find yourself left in the lurch. 'You must always be ahead; then there is no chance or time to control yourself exactly at the moment of spring.'

What in fact Mancinelli is implying is that he rides by instinct and if in doing so he breaks certain basic rules, who is to criticise when one considers the remarkable successes that he has achieved? These include The Daily Mail Cup, London (1961, 1967), the Grand Prix, Nice, Madrid and Rome (1963), Grand Prix, Aachen (1966) and an Olympic Gold Medal, 1972. It has been said that Winkler is his hero and that he has tried to mould himself on him; to the ordinary observer there is little similarity. But Winkler, different from most of the German riders, and Mancinelli, certainly different from the d'Inzeos or the other outstanding Italian rider Vittorio Orlandi, both reflect the influences of Caprilli, often referred to as the 'father of show jumping', the undisputed progenitor of the forward seat and without doubt the greatest influence on riding over fences, not least in Italy. His death in a riding accident before he reached his fortieth birthday was a tragedy and disaster for the horse world, but riders such as the d'Inzeos, Allesandro Bettoni, Orlandi and Mancinelli as well as the greatest the world over, have carried on his work. One measure of his genius is reflected in the vast number of successes enjoyed by the thirty-five-year-old Mancinelli, whose school can now be regarded as Italy's national school.

ABOVE *Raimondo d'Inzeo and Posillipo; a less flamboyant style than Mancinelli perhaps but no less effective.*

171

Holland

Nederlands Hippisch Centrum
Deurne

Holland

Holland's up-to-date national riding school is in north Brabant, an area where many British troops were concentrated in the last war. It is a flat stretch of moors, woods and reedy ponds. The big towns of Eindhoven, Tilleberg and Reda provide plenty of industrial wealth, but outside the towns there are many thousands of acres of dairy farming.

Deurne, the home of the National Riding School, is a charming, neat, small country town. Approached by one of the straight tree-lined roads, so typical of Holland, the school is hidden from view by woodland and shrubs. The buildings themselves have a pleasing unity; although utilitarian in design they manage a certain aesthetic appeal. The indoor school is spacious and airy (twenty-five by sixty-five metres), cleverly planned to ensure good, shadow-free lighting from the north in the arena itself. There is also a gallery running the full length of the school where more than two hundred spectators can be comfortably accommodated. A bar at the top end overlooks the school and includes a self-service cafeteria area. There is throughout a friendly, almost hearty atmosphere generated by the riders and their friends.

Jan Bardoel, the director of the school, is still a young man. He notes the importance of the inevitable social side of riding in Holland; it always plays a not inconsiderable part in Dutch sports, since Dutch people love a convivial atmosphere, a drink and a chat, with the result that anything in the nature of a riding school is almost invariably associated with a club and a bar.

The school reflects Holland's character in almost every way. Particularly noticeable about the whole complex is its 'one-ness' for it is possible to walk under cover from the indoor school to the stables and hostel block. In a country where space is at a premium, much thought has been given to how it can best be used; in a school where students not only learn to ride, but also must share the responsibility for the all-round care and maintenance of the horses and amenities there is no room for extravagance. Everything is designed with economy and practicality in mind. In the stables there are non-slip floors, and small but well-equipped tack rooms cater for groups of looseboxes where up to forty-six horses can be kept. The boxes are of generous proportions.

Attached to this area is the hostel block with rooms accommodating at most three, but more usually two students, on comfortable bunks one

PREVIOUS PAGES *The spacious indoor school at Deurne is cleverly planned to ensure good, shadow-free lighting.*

The main stable block, designed like the rest of the school, with economy and practicality in mind. The floors are non-slip and the looseboxes are grouped around small well-equipped tack rooms.

above the other. There are excellent shower and toilet facilities and a well-equipped gymnasium.

In addition, there are lecture rooms with slide projectors, a miniature cinema and a small library. Mr Bardoel is emphatic in his belief that physical fitness as well as mental awareness are vital parts in the training of a rider; this is a point that does not appear to be so generally appreciated in the majority of even the more important riding schools the world over.

Outside, a terrace forms an excellent viewing-point over the large grass and sandy areas where outdoor show jumping, competitions and training are held. In the woodlands surrounding the school there are also cross-country fences and tracks, the whole area being so large in acreage that it is possible to run a full scale three-day event at Deurne. There are thirteen hectares of ground immediately around the school, and more than three hundred hectares in all, consisting mainly of forests.

The school was founded in the summer of 1969, thanks largely to the energy and determination of Colonel Schummelketel, who has always been interested in the advancement of riding knowledge among young people and is himself a distinguished journalist, being editor of *De Hoefslag*, the Dutch horse journal. Before the war, riding in Holland was mainly the preserve of army officers and farmers; the former ceased to ride after the Second World War, though for many years it was from the army, as in other countries, that the best instructors came. The farmers, however, have continued to have a great influence on riding in the country through their clubs, although it became quite obvious in the sixties that with the increase of leisure riding there was a real demand for a national school.

The Dutch Sports Federation, which covers every branch of sport, is dedicated to providing national centres for all sports and was, therefore, quickly persuaded that its help – in cash and in kind – was needed for a Dutch riding centre. The cost of the centre was 1,600,000 guilders (£250,000; $625,000), of which the Sports Federation provided 300,000 guilders, the government 500,000 guilders, the rest coming from industry and enthusiastic individuals. Thus one-third came from the government via the Ministry of Agriculture; a large proportion came from the Dutch equivalent of the tote (and indeed one-fifth of the annual turnover each

OPPOSITE *The school at Deurne opened in 1969 and already is influencing standards of Dutch international equestrianism, by ensuring an increasingly dependable reservoir of good young riders available for selection.*

year is supplied by the tote). The school took eighteen months to be built and was officially opened in July 1969 by Prince Bernhard of the Netherlands. The running costs amount to 1,200 guilders – rather less than £200 ($500) – per pupil per month, for which the pupil can keep his horse and himself at the school. Of this sum the pupil pays only 500 guilders – a little over £20 ($50) per week – but this is still a considerable sum. The rest comes from the government fund raised by the levy on gambling.

Though this government support certainly sounds generous, Mr Bardoel is of the opinion that the subsidy is still not enough to allow less well-off people to attend the school and would like to see it greatly increased. Unfortunately the Dutch Government, like many others, still regards riding as something of an élite sport reserved for the comparatively wealthy.

The school has no horses of its own; all students or pupils must bring their own horses. There are four instructors and two veterinary surgeons. The chief instructor is Jan Terranea, his assistants being Jan Schrueder, Ulke van Meeteren and Hans Wiegersma. The veterinary surgeons at the present time are Dr Laveaux and Dr Jeuitse. All course-building is under the supervision of Colonel Schummelketel. In addition to courses in straightforward equitation, courses are held in the management of riding schools, book-keeping, veterinary work and stable management, creating a commendably comprehensive programme.

In all, teachers and instructors, including the part-time ones, amount to about ten, but there are no grooms as all students take care of their own horses. Mr Bardoel, who took over in 1971 and who previously worked with a big chemical firm, is of the opinion that many people in the horse world tend to be too narrow-minded, and he is keen to broaden the basis of the courses at all levels. He considers his experience in industry to be a great help in his present job, believing that horsey people generally tend to be somewhat impractical. In fact his father bred horses so he does come from a 'horsey' background.

In one year the school has an average of thirty-five full-time pupils. Before a pupil can come to the school, he must have one year of practice in a riding school, thus getting used to the routine of all work connected with horses – early rising and hard work. At eighteen the young rider can come to the centre for the admission examinations. There is then a first

OPPOSITE *Evening at Deurne; the end of a hard day's work.*
OVERLEAF *There are no grooms at Deurne, students must take care of their own horses and tack. They do everything themselves, including waiting at table in the canteen and washing up.*

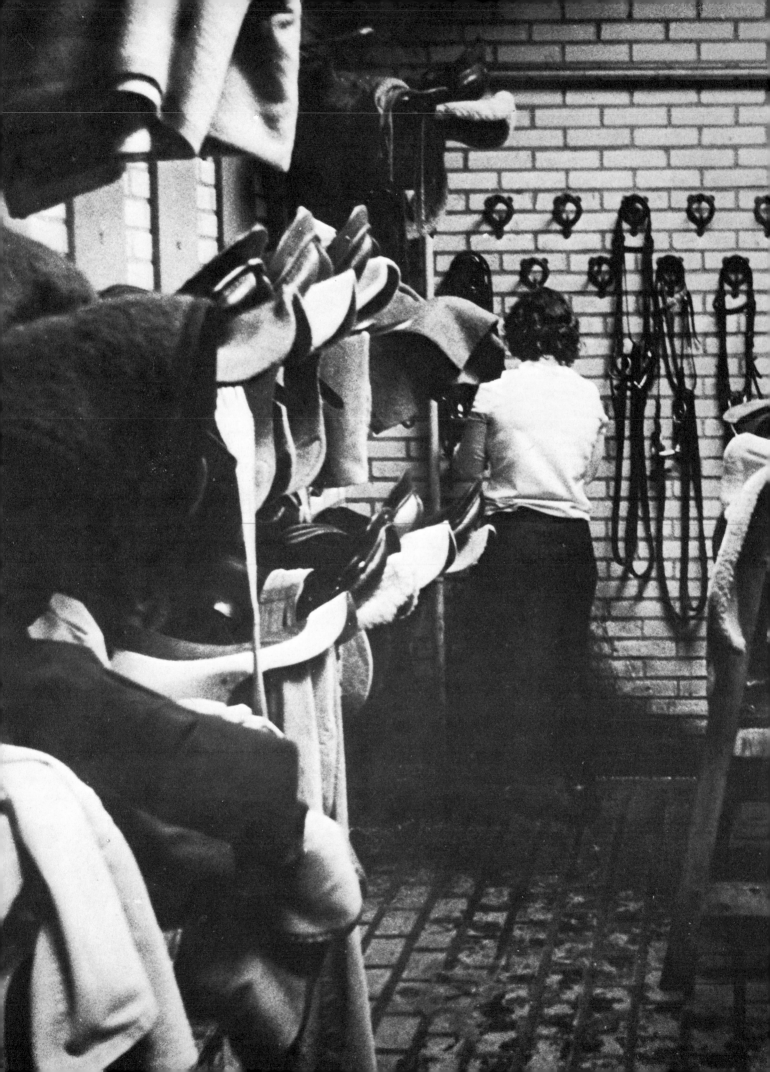

ABOVE AND OPPOSITE *The school has an average of thirty-five full-time students each year taking part in the instructors' courses. In the woodlands surrounding the school, permanent fences and tracks provide useful cross-country training and there are several grassed and sandy paddocks for schooling over show jumps.*

course of three months, mainly involving stable management and basic riding control. Next, for nine months, he goes to a riding school anywhere in the country for practical experience. A second three months at the centre follows which brings a young student to the level of assistant instructor. Then comes another period of nine months of practical work at an outside riding school; back to the centre for the Instructor Third Class qualification (which involves book-keeping, etc.). Finally, exceptionally talented people in this group can stay at the centre for a further year for Instructor Second Class certificates. To reach the Instructor First Class certificate, the full course extends to five years, but so far in Holland there are no first-class instructors and only two second-class instructors. With this new programme, however, a pupil can start at the age of seventeen, begin his career at eighteen, become an instructor at twenty-one and, if particularly talented, by the time he is twenty-seven or twenty-eight, he can be a first-class instructor. Each year there are four separate courses held at the school; approximately 150 people enter for the admission exams, of whom only a small proportion can be accepted. By the end of 1973 some fifty pupils had reached the level of Instructor Third Class.

In addition, the training of the Dutch Olympic riders takes place at the National Riding Centre. Before Munich top foreign instructors were imported for the Olympic training. The Dutch show jumpers have also taken part in training courses at Deurne, so although the school is comparatively young, its impact has already been felt in Dutch equestrianism. After the war, riding, and particularly competitive riding, went through rather a lean period in Holland, but there is no doubt that there is an enthusiasm there similar to that in other countries, and it is fortunate indeed that the farmers' clubs kept riding going and were able to provide the background and foundations for a national school. The chief debt, however, is due to Colonel Schummelketel, who has shown such immense determination; it was not easy at the beginning, either in getting the plan accepted and off the ground or, in the early days, persuading people that it was either necessary or useful. However, thanks to the government support, it does now seem to be fully established. It is noticeable, too, how the performance of Dutch riders in international competitions has improved over the last few years. There can be no doubt that this is due to the fact that there is an increas-

OPPOSITE *After a training session, a student performs a heart test. Veterinary work forms part of the comprehensive programme at Deurne.*

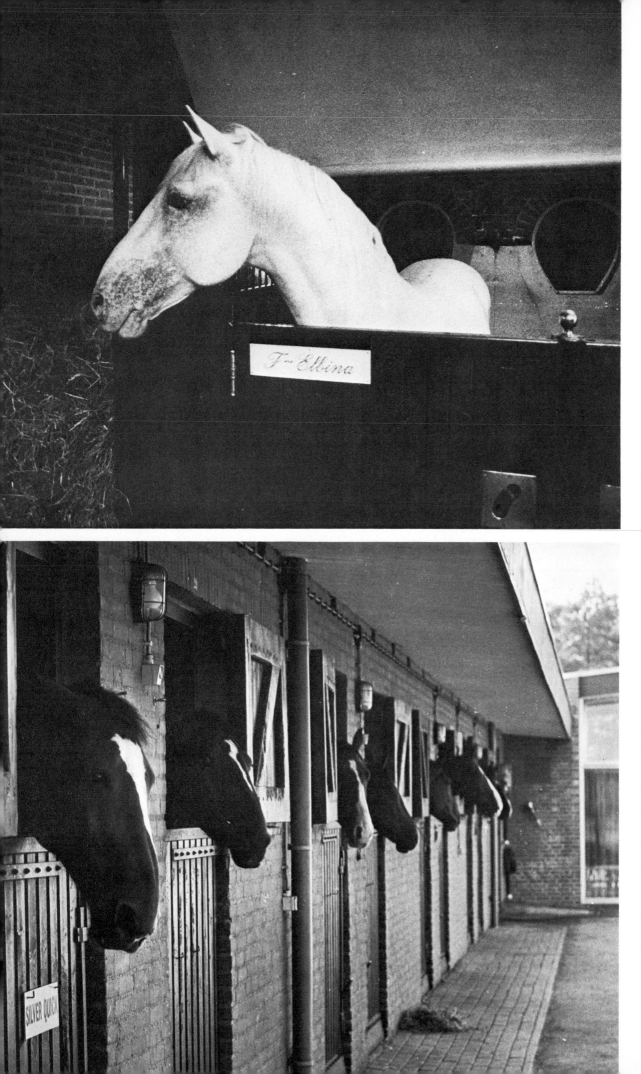

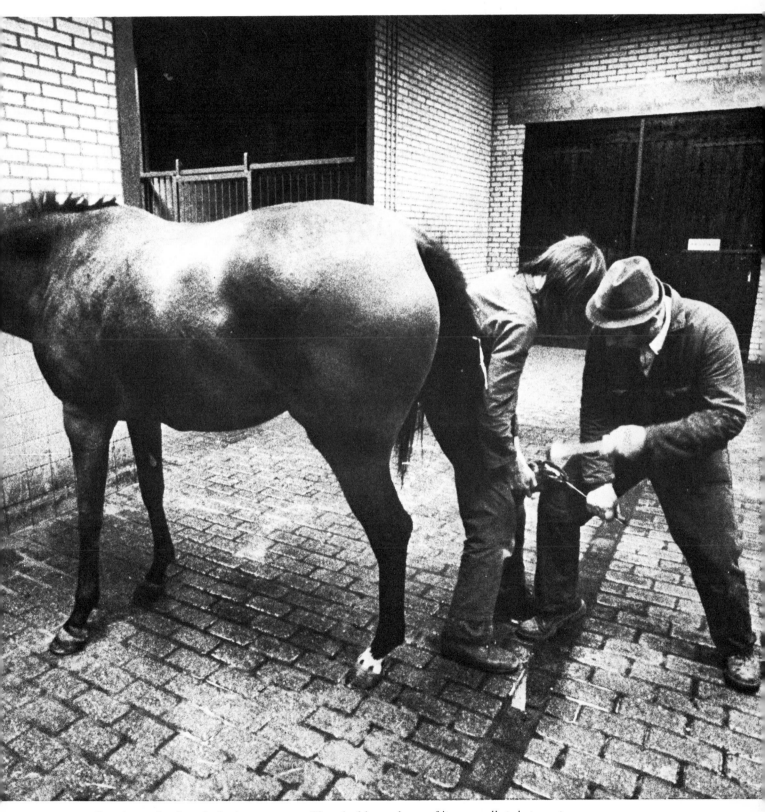

ABOVE *Some instruction from the farrier.* OPPOSITE *The school has no horses of its own; all students must bring their own. Forty-six horses can be accommodated in all.*

ingly dependable reservoir of good young riders making themselves available for international competition, and this without doubt is due to the fact that the standard of instruction in Holland has increased enormously since the foundation of Deurne in 1969. Obviously as a steady flow of qualified instructors come out of Deurne, so the standard will improve even more.

Deurne is of particular interest in that it is a national centre that was started from scratch not in any way being built up on a school, an organisation or a firm local tradition already in existence. As such its progress has been remarkable and worthy of the highest praise and admiration. There are nations in Europe that can be considered more horsey, but few national establishments enjoy greater enthusiasm and dedication.

OPPOSITE, ABOVE AND OVERLEAF *The Dutch Olympic riders come to the Deurne National Centre to train and here one of the van Doorne sisters, both of whom are members of the dressage team, demonstrates the half pass to the left and work at the canter on a circle of ten metres diameter for the benefit of the students.*

Great Britain

The National Equestrian Centre
Stoneleigh

Great Britain

The riding public in Britain has increased fivefold over the past twenty years, riding schools have multiplied and membership of the British Horse Society has rocketed from 4,000 in 1947 to over 25,000 in 1975.

It had been clear for many years that a national equestrian 'university' was needed – a centre with facilities for training instructors, for producing top-class riders who could go on to represent the country in the equestrian sport, for holding many and varied courses at all levels, for conferences and so on. The offices of the British Horse Society and the British Show Jumping Association at Bedford Square, London, had long been uncomfortable, overcrowded and inadequate, having to accommodate the entire administrative complex of the country's burgeoning equestrian organisations and stores.

In August 1965 the executive committee of the British Horse Society felt that it would be advisable to move out of London, and a committee was formed to investigate the possibility of accepting an offer from the Royal Agricultural Society of a plot of land on their show ground. The parcel of land at the agricultural centre at Stoneleigh, near Kenilworth in Warwickshire, proved ideal for the offices and indoor riding school which were to be the nucleus of a national equestrian centre.

To finance this large undertaking three hundred founder members of the National Equestrian Centre, a group which included Her Majesty the Queen, were asked to donate a hundred guineas each. This sum of about £30,000 ($75,000) was brought up to the final £70,000 ($175,000) needed to build the school and office blocks by a loan from the British Show Jumping Association and one, interest free, from a member of the British Horse Society, the sale of the lease at Bedford Square and a substantial government grant. Thanks largely to John Tilke, owner of a large riding establishment at Stratford-upon-Avon and a member of the B.H.S. Council, many of the contractors and suppliers involved in the building of the school were prepared to work or sell their materials at cost or less and construction expenses were reduced to manageable proportions.

As Honorary Director of the Centre I cut the first turf in January 1967, and after an astonishingly brief period of twenty-one months, the first and second stages of an ambitious plan were completed. The co-operation between planners, constructors, architects and decorators was a unique

PREVIOUS PAGES *Stoneleigh's new stable block; permanent stabling for two hundred horses has now been provided.* OPPOSITE *Colonel Bill Froud, national instructor during Stoneleigh's first years, taking a class in the indoor school.*

example of how work can be carried out by dedicated people. In fact the office block designed to house the B.H.S. and the B.S.J.A., which had previously shared offices in London, was ready for occupation by May 1967, just five months after the start of building operations. The administration moved to Stoneleigh the same month.

The immediate advantage of the move was that a single identity was created – the National Equestrian Centre. Although not designed to diminish the identity of either the British Horse Society or the British Show Jumping Association it is, with its all-embracing activities, more easily understood by the public, particularly because of its single geographically central location. The object of the new centre is to function more efficiently than had been possible in the cramped quarters in London and to raise the standard of riding throughout the country by training instructors. Although this takes priority it does not preclude the training of ordinary riders. The Centre offers groups and societies a site where they can further their own specialist interests, and a central location where horses can be schooled under the supervision of experts. Every member of the British Horse Society, the British Show Jumping Association, the Pony Clubs and all affiliated riding schools may use the school and its facilities. Other organisations may also use the school for demonstrations, instruction, conference and show purposes.

The bodies principally associated with the centre are:

THE BRITISH SHOW JUMPING ASSOCIATION
The B.S.J.A. is responsible for the sport of show jumping and frames its rules in Britain. Its stated objectives are:
1   To improve the standard of jumping
2   To provide for the representation of Great Britain in international competitions
3   To prescribe the general standard and height of obstacles for show jumping
4   To promote and encourage the holdings of shows where jumping competitions are held
5   To make rules for the judging of jumping competitions
6   To arrange the registration of horses and ponies
7   To record the results and winnings of horses and ponies in show jumping competitions

OPPOSITE *Ann Moore, Women's European Champion in 1971, was herself a student at Stoneleigh on frequent occasions. Her father, Norman Moore, is Chairman of the Centre.*

Great Britain

THE BRITISH HORSE SOCIETY

The role of the B.H.S. is to encourage high standards of horsemanship and horsemastership and to promote the welfare of horses and ponies. The B.H.S. is the national body responsible for equitation. Recognised as such by the government it protects the interests of horsemen and works for the improvement and expansion of riding facilities all over the country. By approving riding schools, publishing books and holding examinations it seeks to improve the standards of horsemastership, instruction and equitation. Membership is open to anyone over seventeen years of age interested in horses and their welfare. The society provides a range of services to stimulate interest in horses and ponies and to help all those who ride or own horses and ponies. It supports the Horse and Pony Breed Societies and all agencies concerned with the welfare of horses and ponies. It is the parent body of the Pony Club and of all affiliated riding clubs.

THE PONY CLUB

The Pony Club is an organisation for young people under twenty-one years of age. Its objects are:

1 To encourage young people to ride and learn to enjoy all kinds of sports connected with horses and riding.
2 To provide instruction in riding and horsemanship and to instil in members the proper care of their animals.
3 To promote the highest ideals of sportsmanship, citizenship and loyalty, thereby cultivating strength of character and self-discipline.

THE RIDING CLUBS

The British Horse Society is responsible for the rules and fixture lists of affiliated dressage and combined training competitions, also one- and two-day horse trials, and three-day events at Badminton and Burghley. The B.H.S. keeps a register of combined training and dressage horses; it also trains dressage judges and arranges courses of instruction for members.

RIDING FOR THE DISABLED

The Riding for the Disabled Association is an autonomous body maintaining close liaison with the British Horse Society. There are groups throughout the United Kingdom offering riding to over 5,500 physically and mentally handicapped children and adults. The equestrian world provides the facilities and the medical authorities select the riders and help those who run the groups.

The above bodies all make full use of the school, which is administered by the British Equestrian Federation of which Colonel Sir Michael Ansell is chairman. The Federation appoints a Board of Management of which, until assuming the chairmanship of the British Horse Society, I had the honour to be chairman. The two main equestrian bodies of the horse world in Britain, the British Horse Society and the British Show Jumping Association, are equally represented and are equally responsible for the costs of running the centre though, happily, since its inception it has each year broken even or made a small profit, which in view of the fact that it gets no direct government grant, but only help with the instructors' and officers' salaries, is a very commendable state of affairs.

The Centre is truly a growing enterprise, its programme expanding yearly. Today Stoneleigh is well on its way to fulfilling the vision of its future described by Colonel Sir Michael Ansell in 1967:

'Let us imagine what we hope to find at Stoneleigh by the mid-seventies when the centre will have been in existence more than five years. From the office building we look towards the west where two hundred yards away stands the massive but not unattractive building of the new indoor riding school. The outside walls are covered with well-clipped creeper and rambling roses. On entering the large double doors we are met with a feeling of brightness and cleanliness. The lighting is excellent from the transparent roof and modern fluorescent light, and the floor is of a light shade of brown.

'The indoor arena itself, sixty-four by twenty-four metres, is sufficiently large for any dressage competition, and even a jumping course could be erected if wanted. On the walls hang large mirrors. (In fact, in 1973 Spillers presented the N.E.C. with one of the largest mirrors in the world, over twenty-two metres in length.) Undoubtedly many a young horseman receives a shock when he sees his reflection in this mirror. Well do I remember my shock when riding with the *Cadre Noir* in Saumur I glanced at myself in a mirror and then at my companions.

'Near the school, on what was once a rough piece of land, there are two *manèges*, each sixty by twenty metres. These were cinder, but now in one of them a new type of synthetic turf, resembling grass, is being tested. These outdoor schools are of particular interest to the small riding school proprietor. They are attractively surrounded by shrubs, with a covered stand on one side to seat fifty. The nearest of the *manèges* is fitted with flood-lighting, and the outside track has a polythene awning to keep horse and rider dry, so that schooling need not stop because of bad weather.

'For competitions and some demonstrations, if not held too near the dates of the Royal Show, the main arena and the two smaller arenas are

OPPOSITE AND ABOVE *A lecture by Bill Froud on the anatomy and care of the horse is illustrated with a detailed structural model.*

always available. Six years ago the main arena was carefully drained, and now it is beginning to look like the famous Wembley turf.

'Many will wish to train for cross-country competitions and the Trustees of the Stoneleigh Estate, with great generosity, have allowed permanent fences to be built on the estate. The course builder, using ingenuity, can plan cross-country courses for both one- and three-day events but, still more important, a field of about five acres has been put aside as a permanent jumping ground where the horseman can find every imaginable fence from a bank to waters of all sizes, railway crossings, double oxers and ditches. In the middle of the field is a circular *manège* for loose jumping, which enables the rider to warm up his horse on the ground before starting to jump. Great attention has been paid to the draining of the landings and take-offs of fences, but owing to the number and variety of obstacles, these fences do not get really poached.

'Having jumped a few fences in the arena the horseman is able to go for a canter down woodland rides jumping back into the arena over a stiff post and rails. To many, this is reminiscent of the mounted sports ground at Aldershot, where our gold medal show jumping team of 1952 trained, as did also the Australian gold medal team in the three-day event of 1960.

'Stabling and living accommodation were already good when the centre was formed in 1967, but the permanent stabling for two hundred is now excellent. The accommodation for the riders – cubicles with good bathrooms – would have been the envy of the subaltern or undergraduate. Stable management must always be improved, and it is hardly surprising to find a "model" yard for twelve horses. Here experiments and trials are carried out with forms of permanent synthetic rubber bedding, automatic drinking troughs: anything to improve the standard of horsemastership and at the same time to reduce the cost of keeping horses. There are unlimited opportunities.

'Here in the centre of England as we look out on the trees, flowering shrubs and the well-kept grass, we have all the facilities for one of the greatest modern equestrian centres, and let us now imagine how the many interests centred on the horse will make full use of these great opportunities, for unless full use is made the centre will fail.

'As already emphasised, the need for instructors is pressing, and Stoneleigh now has a permanent instructional staff. The British Horse

OPPOSITE *A jumping class in the indoor school. Mirrors hanging the length of the school can help students to correct their style.*

Society will be careful not to permit overheads to cripple this centre in early days, as was the case of St George's some years ago. A small cadre will be formed under a chief national instructor, whose duties will be to organise instruction. He will be based at Stoneleigh, but will travel on lecturing and organising courses for "would-be" instructors throughout the United Kingdom. Further, he will be visiting Europe in search of more information.

'At Stoneleigh there will be a permanent staff in residence under the assistant national instructor. This staff will consist of four apprentice instructors, and these will be of great importance in the future. They will be carefully selected, and they should be aged between twenty and twenty-three, holders of the Preliminary Instructors' Certificate, good horsemen or horsewomen, prepared to continue teaching; above all they should possess the personality and looks of horsemen.

'It is hoped to produce a new instructors' certificate, falling between the Fellowship and the British Horse Society Instructors' Examination. This will be known as the British Horse Society Special Instructors' (Practical) Examination, and is to be aimed at people with the ability to teach future instructors. Apprentice instructors on the staff at Stoneleigh will be expected to qualify as Special Instructors after their two years' training. This new class can give incentive to the many now instructing at approved riding schools. The examination will be held at Stoneleigh, where the candidate will appear before the examiners for three or four days.

'Horses will, of course, be required for demonstration purposes, and it might be expected that the centre will be ready to accept a limited number of horses belonging to members for training. Each apprentice instructor should have at least two trained horses and a third half-trained. This requirement is based on the system at the cavalry school at Weedon. The British Horse Society will not need to purchase its own horses, as undoubtedly some members will be only too pleased to leave their horses in the hands of these young apprentice instructors for schooling.

'On the permanent staff there will be a stud groom with three or four strappers, and apart from demonstrating grooming they will be responsible for the instructors' horses. Although the assistant national instructor will always be at the centre, the apprentice instructors will be out during

Two shire teams chain-harrowing in the indoor school.

the summer helping at Pony Club camps. The centre will be administered by the secretary-general of the British Horse Society, and it is hoped that he will not find it difficult to arrange time for the many groups to have use of the centre, for the demand will become such that there is never a spare day. That is as it must be, for if the centre is to be self-supporting, like an aeroplane, it must be permanently in use.

'There will be conferences of riding school proprietors who will meet to study and hear the latest developments in teaching and the management of riding schools. These members will have the opportunity to hear experts not only on the subject of equitation, but on accountancy, building and estate management. The centre will always be available for conferences of those interested in the horse or pony, and surely during the week of the Royal Show the fine outdoor riding school will become a stage where visitors from overseas may see our horses and ponies at their best. One morning Welsh ponies may fill the stage, whilst an expert explains the finer points of the breed and, even more important, where the best animals can be found. Later there may be a display explaining the pleasure of trekking, and where to go for a trekking holiday. From this, the onlooker may hear about driving, or perhaps there will be a demonstration and explanation on how to judge hunters. It is certain that a carefully planned programme will provide the opportunity for visitors to find out anything and everything connected with horses from buying one, to ordering a pair of boots or breeches and, most important, where to learn to enjoy both the breeches and the horse.

'By the mid-seventies the visitor to Stoneleigh will find something of interest going on, whether it be in winter or summer, and, should he or she have a spare moment, there will always be the museum or library where still more may be learnt.'

With few exceptions these prophecies of Sir Michael Ansell have come to fruition. The school is attended by about four thousand people each year and could be described as just about playing to capacity. The director of the centre, Major-General Jack Reynolds, is an exceptionally able administrator and the national instructor for the first five years of the centre's existence was Colonel Bill Froud who was ideally suited to the job. Experts in different fields of equitation are invited to take courses which are generally of four or five days' duration, though longer courses are now being included in the curriculum, notably the course on horsemanship and horsemastership for apprentice jockeys.

The hub around which the activities of the centre revolve is the indoor riding school, construction of which began immediately after the offices were completed. Today it is certainly one of the most modern and fully-equipped riding schools in Britain, not to say the world. The ring itself, large enough for a full-size course of twelve jumps (it is slightly larger than the ring at the Empire Pool, Wembley) is surfaced with sand and wood shavings, slightly salted to retain moisture. Overhead a Filon plastic roof of unique design allows a diffused, shadowless light through to the ring.

Running the length of the ring is the gallery, equipped with upholstered tip-up seats, many of which have been given by Pony Club branches from all over the world whose names are attached to the seats.

Great Britain

Photographs of the nine pony breeds indigenous to the British Isles line the kicking boards in the indoor school.

A number of approved riding schools have generously contributed towards the cost of the kicking boards. Those breed societies that have undertaken to provide an area of the panel under the gallery have a large picture of their specific breed mounted on the panel and the hunts of Britain have contributed to the glass panels in the arcade.

None of this would have come into being if it had not been for the outstanding donations from these riding clubs, industry and private sources: a hostel was given by the Royal Agricultural Society; a modern stable block by the Worshipful Company of Saddlers, the lecture room equipped with cine projector and closed-circuit television for instructional purposes by the wineshippers Martini and Rossi Ltd; first-aid room by Ronald Margolin, a well-known exhibitor at horse shows; a conference room by the brewers, Whitbread and Co. Ltd. Gifts of furnishings from the journal *Horse and Hound* have created a most luxurious study and library; the Diamond Bar Riding Centre in California generously donated the funds to fit out a canteen. Even the paint was presented by the Blue Circle Cement Co. and the overall interior was designed without charge by Tibor Reich of Stratford-upon-Avon. Stoneleigh has come into existence only through this extraordinary national support. They have guaranteed the existence of a centre where people involved with every aspect of the horse can work – from instructors to jockeys; from juniors to top-class international competitors. With the growing emphasis on education and instruction it is hoped that it will become a still greater influence on and help to riding in Great Britain.

Despite the existence of the National Equestrian Centre at Stoneleigh there is still, as yet, no accepted 'school' or tradition as far as British riding is concerned. While the Cavalry School at Weedon existed there was an accepted style and standard of equitation. Since its demise during the Second World War nothing has fully replaced it. Down the years, however, certain firm precepts have been accepted. These have been set out by Colonel V. D. S. Williams who died in 1973. According to Colonel Handler, he was 'the one who has so long been successfully in charge of all the activities of the British horse world and its progress'. His words sum up the best of British thinking on equitation. Though written more than twenty years ago they have never previously been published, but formed part of a lecture given in the early fifties to the now defunct British Riding Club at St George's School, Winkfield,

which it was hoped would develop into a national centre. Ahead of its time and therefore unable to muster sufficient funds and support, it lasted only a few years.

'The purpose of training a horse is to be able to go where one wants, when one wants and how one wants with a minimum of exertion and effort on the part of the rider and with a maximum of ease and, therefore, of preservation on the part of the horse.

'The degree of training depends on the end which the rider wishes to obtain and the work that he requires from his horse. For example, the military horse must be trained to carry different riders under a variety of circumstances; they must go in formation or singly; they must be able to carry a heavy weight for many hours and they must be able to go across country. For economic reasons they must be so trained that they will give useful service for as many years as possible. With the hunter, however, the main thing most people require is that he should be able to gallop and jump; that he should have courage and constitution. The former, therefore, must go through a course of physical and mental training, whereas with the latter it is more innate qualities that are required than training.

ABOVE AND OPPOSITE *Michael Cresswell on Jacapo and Caroline Bradley on Franco, two of Britain's international riders in action at Stoneleigh.*

Great Britain

'The High School rider wishes to train his horse to do all the classical school movements in complete harmony between horse and rider whereas the circus rider wishes to show to a public that does not understand too much about riding a number of effective and brilliant tricks and movements.

'The former (the High School horse) can only be obtained by a comprehensive course of training, whereas the latter (the circus horse) can be obtained much more quickly by artificial movements which, for the sake of sheer display, sacrifice that harmony between horse and rider which is so essential in the former. But no matter what the destination, where time and good riders are available, a proper course of training can only be of advantage to the horse, besides proving a great source of pleasure to its eventual owner. On the other hand, if the training is done in haste and by riders who do not understand what they are doing, more harm than good is done.

'THE TRAINING OF THE RIDER

Before discussing the training of the horse, it is necessary to discuss the training of the rider. In practical teaching of riding a number of important problems cannot be handled owing to lack of opportunity. Yet it is important for the pupil to understand these problems in order that he may understand the difference between theory and practice and avoid the difficulties that arise from trying to obtain the impossible from himself and his horse.

'THE CORRECT SEAT

The three principles of a good seat are: balance, looseness and the ability to follow the movements of the horse. To tell the rider how to hold his limbs or to copy a stereotyped seat is inclined to lead to stiffness, which is the one fault which we wish to avoid. Nevertheless the rider must sit well down in the lowest part of his saddle with the weight of his body resting vertically on two pelvic bones and the fork – the three points of support. The seat should be maintained chiefly by balance, grip only being resorted to when balance is lost or to prevent the loss of balance. Arms and legs have nothing to do with balance and should be left free so that they can apply the aids correctly.

Ann Moore on Fair Game competing in a Grade 'B' and 'C' class at the centre.

'EXERCISES FOR BRACING THE BACK

In foreign schools great importance is paid to the use of back muscles. The correct use of the back muscles must be thoroughly understood: it is just the reverse of sticking out the buttocks and hollowing the back. On a swing the back is braced for the forward swing and slackened for the backwards swing. If you sit on a chair, leaning against the back, you can slide your buttocks forward by bracing the back. If you straddle a stool and sit right on the edge, you can tilt it forward by bracing the back muscles, but to do this, the legs from the knee downwards must be behind the perpendicular and to the sides.

'BRACING THE BACK ON HORSEBACK

The same movement as practised on the ground must now be practised on the horse's back. It is essential for the rider thoroughly to understand this movement in order to be able to stick to his horse – sit down in the saddle – follow the movements of the horse – and "feel".

'FEEL

From the beginning, the rider must be taught to "feel" the movements of his horse with his seat. When the horse stands unevenly on his hind legs, the rider shifts about in order to lever himself up. He must be taught to realise why. Trotting on different diagonals is a good exercise in feeling.

'THE CENTRE OF GRAVITY

The rider must always keep his centre of gravity directly over that of his horse. By this the rider is able to control the movements of his horse with as little exertion as possible and the horse is best able to deal with the rider's weight. A good example of this: the porter easily carries the heavy trunk on his shoulders when its centre of gravity is directly above that of his own. The law of balance can best be explained in terms of a juggler. When he stands still he holds his staff vertically, when he moves forward he inclines the staff forward and the faster he moves the more he inclines it.

The horse is allowed to stretch out freely over the fence, the rider moving forward in the saddle in line with the horse's centre of gravity.

'THE BALANCED SEAT

When the horse moves forward the rider must move his centre of gravity forward so as to remain in balance. At the same time he must maintain his seat on the three points of support. To combine these two movements is difficult: if the rider leans his trunk forward he must raise his pelvic bones from the saddle. The critical moment is at the beginning of the movement, when there is danger of being left behind.

'If the principle of bracing the back is adhered to, the rider presses his horse forward by pushing his buttocks and, therefore, his whole centre of gravity forward. The result is a very close contact with the horse and the rider avoids being left behind or raising his pelvic bones from the saddle.

'As the pace increases, the difficulty of maintaining both the seat on the three points of support and the centre of gravity in harmony with that of the horse increases, until in the extended trot the rider is forced to "post" and in the gallop the rider abandons his seat in the saddle and takes his support on the knees and stirrups, resting his hands on his horse's neck.

'POSITION OF THE HANDS
Generally too much importance is paid to the position of the hands. The movement which the hands execute in order to give the aids should be slight and be confined to almost imperceptible twists of the wrists. All aids, even those for turning, should mainly emanate from the seat. It is utterly wrong to attempt any change of direction by the reins alone. This is driving not riding.'

Although it would be idle to pretend that from the start the National Centre had the support of the whole horse world – or even of all members of the two principal societies involved – it has become increasingly accepted, and its value appreciated. Its courses range wider every year, thus providing an expanding service not only for members of the two societies, but for the many riders who belong, regrettably, to no society. (It is estimated that some two million people ride in Britain: the total membership of the two societies, including the riding clubs and pony clubs, is in the order of 100,000.) There is little doubt that the membership of the B.H.S. and the B.S.J.A. which has nearly doubled since 1965, is due to the existence of a National Centre. The National Equestrian Centre is still in its early days and there are great opportunities for development. But I believe that in the years to come it will be recognised as a centre of great importance.

National Hunt jockeys, more accustomed to the formidable fences and pace of steeplechasing, try their skill at show jumping in a special annual competition at Stoneleigh. Regular eight-week courses for apprentice jockeys are run in association with the Tote Levy Board.

ABOVE *An entrant in the donkey show.*
OPPOSITE *The many courses at Stoneleigh include one for R.S.P.C.A. inspectors which covers the care and handling of horses in harness.*

The National Equestrian Centre, Stoneleigh

West Germany

The Deutsche Reitschule and
The Deutsches Olympiade Komitee
für Reiterei, Warendorf

West Germany

At the European Three-Day Event Championships in Kiev in 1973, the West German equestrian team led from start to finish. They retrieved the champion's crown which had remained beyond their grasp since 1959 at Harewood. This brilliant success must be due in part to the intensive training given at the national equestrian centre in Warendorf.

West Germany appears to be the only nation in Europe – and that includes Britain – which has had the foresight and the good sense to build a special training school for its potential Olympic riders, while it has, in addition, developed a national riding school devoted to improving the standard of riding generally and to producing top-class instructors specifically. This policy has undoubtedly paid off, even in the field of three-day eventing, in which the West Germans till now have not been really strong. Special attention is being paid to this sport at Warendorf and the results over the last year or two have obviously greatly improved.

Warendorf is a small town, not far from Munster, in Westphalia, a flat and not especially beautiful area. Large coniferous forests are scattered here and there, interspersed with stretches of pasture land and heath. Although dairy and beef farming are now the mainstay of the area, horse breeding has always been important. Indeed, horse breeding is Westphalia's greatest tradition, and under the circumstances it is not surprising that Warendorf was chosen as the home of the National Riding School. The Westphalian Stud is associated with the riding school and shares its premises.

There are three important riding schools in Warendorf. The oldest is the Deutsche Reitschule (the National Riding School) and the newest is the Olympic School run by the Deutsches Olympiade Komitee für Reiterei. The third school is a military riding academy which occupies a barracks with stables and training facilities, used in earlier times for the training of Olympic teams. The army took this over towards the end of the 1960s, hence new premises had to be found. However, the need for specialised Olympic training with first-class modern facilities had already existed and this was the main impetus in building the new school.

The contrast in appearance between the Deutsche Reitschule and the Olympic School reflects their very different characters. The Olympic School, which is on the edge of the town with easier access to open

PREVIOUS PAGES *The stables of the Deutsche Reitschule.*

*Horse breeding is Westphalia's greatest tradition so Warendorf is an appropriate
home for the National School and a stud which maintains native breeds
such as the Leichte Kaltblüter as well as thoroughbred stock.*

country, is a much more modern and certainly more functional building, of no great aesthetic appeal. The Deutsche Reitschule, on the other hand, is nearer the centre of the town. It has stabling and offices which are partly modern but which also include some very old buildings, allegedly used at one time as a monastery. The exercise areas and *manèges* are flanked by austere brick buildings which endow the school with an air of permanence and dignity. Outside the stables there are spacious facilities for schooling, a sand *manège* for dressage, a covered area for schooling horses on the lunge, and an outside show jumping ring. There is an impressive parade ground, mainly for use by the stallions and their uniformed attendants, but also used by the riders themselves. In addition, there is a cross-country course with tracks and hacking facilities, though this is some distance from Warendorf in the countryside.

The director of the Deutsche Reitschule is Günther Festerling, whose reputation extends far beyond Warendorf. There is no doubt that the school is fortunate to have Herr Festerling as its head. Though he is a cheerful and extrovert character, he is nevertheless firm, decisive and a disciplinarian. He is a man of considerable vision, great ability and real authority. Very much at the centre of things at Warendorf, he has his office on the ground floor of the administration building, which was built in 1950. The first floor includes the academic area and well-equipped classrooms including, among other things, models illustrating equine anatomy, all types of show jumping fences set out on boards, as course design and the siting of fences are part of the course, and visual aids such as projectors, films and slides. One of the classrooms overlooks the large indoor school which is twenty-five by eighty-five metres with a grandstand section for spectators.

The number of horses kept at the National School varies between fifty and seventy. This is in addition to the stallions which are also housed there. The stables, though dating from the last century, are still first-rate, with lofty ceilings and spacious centre aisles flanked by loose boxes made of heavy timber with iron railings. Compared with the offices, they are a little old-fashioned, but the whole place is spotlessly clean.

Many riders who were later to achieve fame have at one time or another been students at the National School. One might just mention Hermann Schridde, the show jumper, and Lütke-Westhues, the three-

OPPOSITE *New arrivals are unloaded by the stud grooms and put through their paces in front of the veterinary surgeon.*

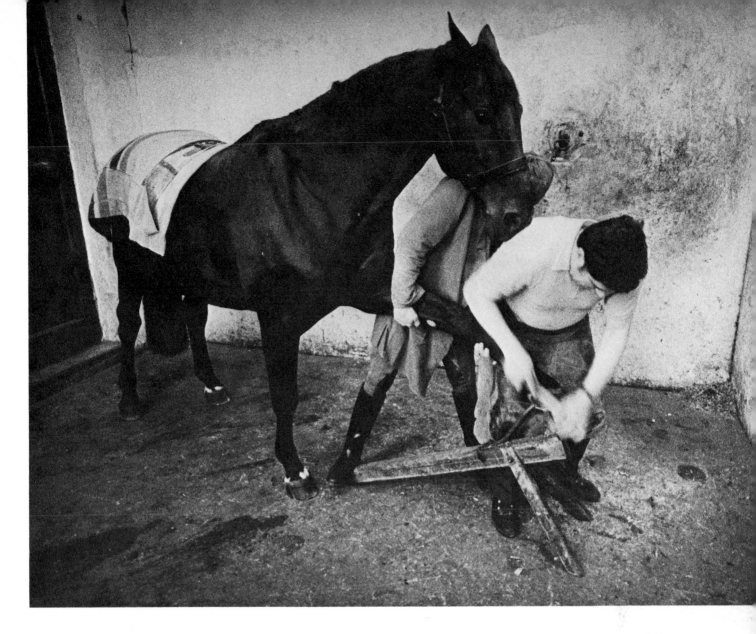

day-event gold medallist at Stockholm in 1956. Well known in British circles is the national hunt amateur and three-day eventer Chris Collins who recently attended a course at Warendorf. These riders owe much to the staff: the director, Herr Festerling, the senior riding instructor and head of stable staff; in addition two veterinary surgeons are attached to the school. There are two commercial teachers, a sports instructor with a diploma and, from time to time, other instructors are brought in for special purposes.

The school does not specialise in any one particular branch of equestrianism because its main goal is to produce riding instructors trained equally well in all subjects. Jumping is no more important than dressage and vice versa. The tendency is not to emphasise the esoteric High School of three-day eventing, but to concentrate on the overall appearance of horse and rider – those things that are applicable to all aspects of riding. Horses must walk properly balanced and stand neatly in the bridle. Absolute obedience – the perfect control that the

OPPOSITE AND ABOVE *The farrier at work*.

rider exercises over the horse – must be displayed at all times. Apart from specialist courses for those amateur and junior riders who want particularly to devote extra attention to show jumping, dressage or eventing everything is taught with the same degree of importance.

Instruction revolves around comparatively short courses usually lasting between two and eight weeks. Students come from every kind of background: wealthy people, not-so-wealthy people, amateurs and professionals, those with their own animals and those who come to learn on the school's horses. There is little class difference today, it seems, in the German riding world. The only drawback at Warendorf is that there are no courses for children.

As Warendorf is the main instruction centre for professional riders it naturally influences the standard of instruction all over West Germany. Courses are held which lead up to special examinations – all with the closest possible co-operation of the government – and it is at Warendorf that these national examinations are held. They are not confined merely to riding, but include special tests for horse-breakers and instructors. There are also courses for those connected with the competitive aspect of the sport: judges, stewards and course-builders. The level of education at Warendorf lies between the state riding and driving schools and the training centre of the German Olympic Committee.

Herr Festerling is well aware of the part the National School can play in this new programme. He sees it as essential that more and more professional riders are provided and he hopes that with Warendorf's support more qualified personnel will be forthcoming to meet increasing demands. There can never be enough teachers, in his opinion, because riding has now become the fastest growing sport in Germany.

Opposite the entrance to the school are the administrative offices for the West German Riding Federation, which controls equestrian sport throughout the country. The National Riding School works closely with this organisation, as well as with the principal state association for riding and driving clubs, and the state administrative organisations for horse trials. The training and sponsoring of professional riders remains the main objective of the school, for the ever increasing number of members in the riding clubs (1959: 74,000, and 1970: 180,000), not to mention the founding of many new clubs and schools, demands special attention. The standard of the average professional rider does not as a rule fully meet the requirements. There had been a long-standing request from many state associations and pressure groups that there should be a professional riders' seminar for the continuous training of these professionals. This has at last been organized. The 'seminars', the first of which was held in the autumn of 1970, aim to become a kind of forum for all interested professional riders, and it is hoped that they will play an important part in retraining applicants from other professions who are interested in taking up a career in riding. At the moment the classical art of riding runs the risk of being watered down more and more by the large numbers within riding circles. So the seminars should be a positive influence in maintaining high standards.

Complementing this there are courses within the state associations specially aimed at qualified amateurs. It is planned that courses for junior riders in dressage and show jumping, for dressage riders, for show jumpers, for three-day-event riders and for lady riders will become a constant part of the training programme at Warendorf.

The shortcomings of the present facilities for top-class competitive training are being felt more and more in the Federal Republic, as elsewhere. The school is trying to avoid this bottleneck by enlarging its training programme for potential competitors. Each year there are to be many training courses to enable all state commissions for horse trials to send their junior riders to the special courses. Those who attend these courses will reach the state-approved level and can go on to train junior riders in their own areas. With the number of pupils approaching five hundred each year, it is obvious that the National School is fulfilling an extremely useful function.

The tone and purpose of the Olympic School are very different. Here riders acquire that final polished brilliance which gives them the edge in international competition. The head of the Olympic School is Alfons Schulze Dieckhoff, whose successes in the international field speak for themselves. Most of the great names in German competitive riding have been, at one time or another, associated with the Olympic School – Fritz Theidemann, for example, who will always be associated with that great horse Meteor (a famous Olympic combination), and Hans Winkler, who has played a major part in the development of Warendorf for many years.

At the Olympic School there are three senior instructors, one for

West Germany

RIGHT *The number of horses at the National School varies between fifty and sixty. All are owned by the government.*
BELOW *Fancy a carrot? Some titbits to be added to the regular feed.*

each of the three main sports. There is the famous Herr Brinkmann, the chief instructor for show jumping and indeed, without doubt, the most eminent designer of show jumping courses in the world today: his courses for the Munich Olympics won the admiration of even the most critical observers. The chief instructor for eventing is Herr Habel, though he is not at Warendorf full-time. In all, the staff totals about fifteen. As only the top twenty riders in the three main elements of competitive riding are eligible for the school, plus a limited number of exceptional juniors, it would seem that this is a remarkably – and enviably – high ratio of staff to students.

The Olympic School runs properly organised courses for students only in the autumn. For the rest of the year the students come in smaller groups with their own horses, to courses of three or four weeks. During the winter these small groups of riders may stay at the school for several months with their own horses, and make use of the excellent facilities.

Forty-three horses are stabled at the Olympic School throughout the

ABOVE *Schooling over fences at the Deutsche Reitschule. The definite groundline on the take-off allows the horse to judge his distance and stand off well.* OPPOSITE *Courses at the Deutsche Reitschule are comparatively short but intensive, aiming to produce instructors trained in all the main branches of equestrianism.*

year. At the National School the horses are provided by the government; at the Olympic School the majority of the horses belong to the riders or to the West German Riding Federation and are simply sent to Warendorf for schooling. There is a large indoor school with seating for three hundred spectators. Everything has been done to ensure the optimum conditions: the lighting is sophisticated, there is a sprinkler system and the windows are opened and shut by a remote-control system. The stables are all on ground-floor level in blocks of looseboxes, some with the horses entirely indoors, though there are a few 'outdoor' boxes. The boxes have sliding doors with metal bars forming the top half and dividing walls; there are non-slip tile floors which lead to neat, well-designed tack rooms. These tack rooms serve small groups of boxes, with areas nearby for tying up horses, grooming, washing and clipping. Outside are attractive lawns and paddocks, bordering on woodland. Hostel accommodation is available for visiting riders and is included in the general lay-out.

The Olympic School is also spectacularly well set up for outdoor training. There is a large outdoor *manège* for dressage, and ample grassed areas for outdoor show jumping with a great variety of fences up to top international standard. There is an event training course, all of which is accommodated in one large, flat paddock, with slopes and gradients artificially constructed so that various obstacles, typical of those encountered in an event cross-country course, can be practised over. There is a formidable array of practice fences: a 'coffin', water jumps, a 'Normandy' bank and all manner of spreads, drops and fly-fences, including a switchback to give horse and rider opportunities to learn to maintain balance over uneven surfaces. This complex is extremely impressive, and obviously helps to achieve excellent results.

Yet while the successes of the Olympic School are enthralling to those who follow the great international riders, the real foundations of German professional riding are laid, as we have seen, in the less spectacular but equally demanding courses for the training of instructors at the Deutsche Reitschule.

One man who plays an extremely important role in Warendorf's equestrian life is Doktor Dietmar Specht – a man of great energy and obviously a first-class administrator. He is also a fine horseman himself. For over three years Specht worked in Berlin and it was not until 1966

The Olympic School provides first-class modern facilities for the specialised training of international riders.

West Germany

that he came to Warendorf and qualified at the National Riding School as a professional riding instructor; he is also a veterinary surgeon. A man of strong personality, he was quickly able to make the German Federation aware of his opinions. He was with the Mexico Olympic team as veterinary surgeon, and there learned about the problems of organising Olympic equestrian events; it was natural that he should play an important role in the organisation of the 1972 Olympics at Munich.

Dr Specht's varied and exhaustive background in all aspects of horsemastership is evident from his description of the programme at Warendorf:

'A candidate for the examination to be an amateur instructor in Germany must be at least nineteen years old. He must have had basic riding training and have acquired the Third Class bronze medal of the German Horse Society. This proves that he has the ability to ride dressage or take a jumping test in the basic class with good results. We also assume that he has taken part in a two- or three-week-long preparatory course before he takes the examination. These preparatory classes usually take place every spring and autumn in ten or twelve riding schools throughout Germany. In these courses lessons are given in subjects important for the examination. The members of the examination board are appointed by the German Horse Society.

'In the examination the rider has to prove his ability to ride dressage from Class A (Beginner) to L (Elementary) standard. In addition, he has to pass a jumping test of Class A standard, and, if possible, also outside riding. He is examined in practical riding; that is, he must give a lesson, in which he has to teach one or more riders dressage and jumping according to the demands of Class A. He must also prove his abilities in lungeing and equestrian acrobatics, very popular in Germany.

'He also takes a theoretical examination in these subjects: he must understand the science of riding. There is also a practical and theoretical examination in horse management and grooming. A veterinary knowledge of horse diseases is required. He must know the organisation of riding in Germany as well as of the regulations concerning riding competitions, training of riders and examinations. Another important subject in his examination is sport in general. Here the rider must demonstrate a thorough knowledge of training, medical, judicial and

OPPOSITE *Morning exercise for the stallions at Warendorf.*
OVERLEAF *At the Deutsche Reitschule the emphasis is laid on basic principles – absolute obedience and perfect control.*

teaching problems. He must also have a basic knowledge of first aid.

'A recognised training centre must have an indoor riding hall of at least twenty by forty metres and an outside school which is furnished with necessary obstacles. The whole set-up has to meet modern standards, and we stress lodging facilities and sanitary installations. The training centre must be capable of teaching the apprentices the art of riding; in other words it must have enough horses that meet the demands of Class L and M in dressage and jumping. Of course, it must also employ a recognised instructor, as apprentices are only allowed to be trained in recognised training centres by recognised instructors.

'In order to become an instructor of professional riders, the applicant must pass the professional instructor's examination with good results. He must have not only the qualities of a good horseman, but also proven qualities of leadership. There is one exception to the rule – riders who are well-known to the public and have had many years' experience can also be recognised as trainers without formally passing the exam. Herr Winkler and Dr Klimke, for example, are recognised trainers. They do a lot of valuable work in the training field.

'To start his career as a professional rider, the student is supposed to have the German equivalent of a US high school diploma or O levels. If he does not have this, a completed training in another vocation will do. If the applicant does not have these qualifications, he must start as an apprentice groom and must pass this two-year period of training, finishing it with good examination results. He may then begin his professional training, which in this case lasts two years instead of three.

'But generally the training period for a professional rider lasts three years. There is an examination at the end of the first year; the final examination is at the end of the third year. The training is approved by the government.

'It would be much too detailed to list all the demands of the three years of apprenticeship. Briefly, the apprentices are trained throughout the instruction period in riding, lungeing, performing equestrian acrobatics, stable and horse management and theoretical subjects. During

OPPOSITE *Jumping in the indoor school at the Deutsche Reitschule.* OVERLEAF *The Olympic School, situated on the edge of the town with easy access to open country, has a large outdoor* manège *for dressage, ample grassed arenas for show jumping and an event training course, with a formidable array of practice fences, among them water jumps and a 'Normandy' bank. A temporary lapse in obedience* (top left). *Boldly into the water* (bottom left). *The rider's weight is too far back as they approach the bank* (top right). *The right contact on the bank* (bottom right).

the second and third year practical teaching methods are added to the curriculum. It may be of interest to specify in more detail the course for the last year as set out in the training and examination regulations:

I PRACTICAL RIDING

There are lessons on a dressage horse every day. The apprentice must learn to ride well on the curb bit. Class L exercises are carried out repeatedly, and he rides daily on a young horse. Weekly jumping if possible, and monthly jumping over Class A or L show jumping obstacles. He must satisfy higher demands for outside riding. The apprentice must furthermore do certain jumping and dressage tests in horse shows and must take part in foxhunting.

At the end of the training period the apprentice must be able to train horses in all disciplines with standards up to Class L. The training is under constant supervision.

2 PRACTICAL TEACHING

Under supervision, the pupil has to act as an assistant instructor in all disciplines up to Class L. In co-operation with the government, booklets have been issued to each labour exchange in Germany on opportunities for careers with horses. Everyone who is interested can find the details of the career of a professional riding instructor.

3 LUNGEING

Weekly lungeing of young and old horses and exhaustive instruction of horses is an important part of the training.

4 EQUESTRIAN ACROBATICS

Occasionally, the applicant has the chance to teach the performing of equestrian acrobatics.

5 STABLE MANAGEMENT

There is daily work in the stable, as in the first year, but in addition he learns about the management of a large stable, with the supervision and personal responsibilities this involves.

6 THEORETICAL INSTRUCTION

Several times a month the various subjects of the first two years are repeated so that the pupil knows them for his examination. The pupil must know the relevant books on the science of riding and instruction.

7   HORSE MANAGEMENT AND HORSE DISEASES
He must know the important sections of the general instructions which are given out by the German Federation.

8   GENERAL KNOWLEDGE
Instruction in correspondence, general outlines of the keeping of accounts, principles of democracy, working rights, social security, assurance policies, prevention of accidents, the guidance of horses on the road, and general knowledge of sports and its rules are included in the rider's professional training.

9   FIRST AID
The apprentice has to take a first aid course at the local Red Cross Organisation.

The examination covers all the subjects just listed. Once again a special course, which lasts several weeks, prepares the apprentice for his examination. All the preparatory courses and examinations are at the National Riding School at Warendorf. This is the only training centre which is allowed to examine the apprentices, and it is our aim to centralise all the training for professional riders there. The composition of the examination board is always the same.

'Pupils who want to be professional riders can begin their vocational training in April or October; therefore there are final examinations twice a year, in March and September. There are about fifty riders every year who qualify.

'Only those riders who have the training that I have just outlined are allowed to take the examination as a professional riding instructor later on. It is assumed that the applicant has pursued his profession for at least five years. During this time he must have worked under a qualified instructor and must also, under his supervision, have given lessons for at least two years. In order to take the examination to be a professional instructor he must prove his ability in training and leading horses in various disciplines up to Class M (Advanced). The candidate must also attend a preparatory course before the examination; only the Westphalian Riding School at Munster and the Deutsche Reitschule at Warendorf are permitted to give these courses.'

A look at the financing of Warendorf should be of interest to riding enthusiasts in other countries. The government contributes about sixty

West Germany

One of Germany's most experienced and successful international riders, Hans Winkler, who with his famous mare, Halla, became a favourite with crowds the world over; seen here riding Skat at the Royal International Horse Show, London.

Winkler receives the World Championship trophy. He won the Championship in 1955 and 1956.

per cent of the total cost, but there are also donations from the general public and various public bodies. An important source of income is the levy of ten pfennigs taken from everyone attending any horse show or equestrian event in Germany; this amounts to nearly £45,000 ($112,500) a year. So it is clear that the German riders start with great advantages in their Olympic training. In Britain, by way of contrast, the money for Olympic training has to be raised from the general public, and a subsidy is then provided by the government for the cost of transport to the Games.

Despite this generally rosy picture of riding in Germany, Warendorf still faces some difficulties. There is the ever-increasing pressure on its facilities, and there is still a shortage of good event horses in Germany – recent successes notwithstanding – and, for this reason, the Germans have been buying potentially good horses from Britain and Ireland. These are kept permanently at Warendorf.

With three major schools in the town, Warendorf is very much the heart of the horse world in West Germany. It is sad, of course, that the magnificent complex built specially at Reim, near Munich, for the 1972 Olympics – perhaps the most modern in the world – is not at Warendorf, especially as Bavaria is not a horse-riding area. Indeed, that wonderful set-up at Reim has scarcely been used since the Olympics. However, Warendorf is wonderfully well-equipped and provides a complex second to none in Europe.

Winkler's trophies and
rosettes are displayed in the
stables at the Olympic School.

249

Gladstone, New Jersey and Morven Park, Virginia

OPPOSITE *In the absence of a national riding school, centres such as Gladstone and Morven Park take the responsibility of maintaining high standards of horsemanship in the United States.*

USA

The equestrian scene in the United States is more loosely organised than in many European countries, and there is no national riding school or centre to impose a uniform style on American riders. In purely practical terms such a centre would probably prove impossible to maintain; the distance students would have to travel to reach the centre, and the expense of building a facility large enough to cater to students from all over the country, would in themselves be prohibitive.

In the absence of any national school, standards for American riding are set and maintained through the influence of the American Horse Show Association, a national body responsible for the rules and conditions governing all recognised horse shows in the United States. The A.H.S.A. also authorises the official judges in the various fields, from hunter classes to dressage and from breed classes to appointment classes. It is, however, a governing organisation: it is not set up to train riders who will, in the truest sense, be the ambassadors of American riding to the world; nor is it equipped to maintain through training the highest standards of the art of horsemanship. These functions are left to be fulfilled by independent organisations – in the true American tradition.

There is no doubt that, internationally, the best known and the most important of all such equestrian organisations in the United States is the US Equestrian Team, whose headquarters are at Gladstone, New Jersey. Gladstone is in the heart of the Essex Hunt country and, in the past, was a very horse-minded community. The estate of Hamilton Farm, some fifty miles west of New York and close to Morristown, Somerville and Far Hills, is owned by the family of James Cox Brady, the recently appointed chairman of the US Jockey Club, and the big house is still occupied by members of the family. It was built originally in 1907, the stables being completed some ten years later.

Previously the U.S.E.T. headquarters had been at Greenwich, Connecticut, on an estate owned by a very elderly man: there was a danger, therefore, that the estate would be sold upon his death, and no longer be available for a training centre for the U.S.E.T. New headquarters had to be found, so in 1960 the Brady family offered Gladstone, and the U.S.E.T. moved there immediately after the Rome Olympic Games. The U.S.E.T. has a long-term lease at a relatively nominal rental, considering the facilities involved.

OPPOSITE *The U.S.E.T. acquired their permanent home at Gladstone, New Jersey, in 1960.*

Neal Shapiro on Sloopy, members of the successful Munich Olympic team in 1972, training at Gladstone.

The country is typical parkland in undulating countryside, with plenty of woods and trees, the whole estate being open for the team to ride on, except of course the cultivated areas.

Gladstone is not a national centre, nor is it wholly independent. The national federation delegates all responsibility for international training

to the U.S.E.T., whose charter states that the objects are to train horses and riders for international competition, Pan-American Games, championships and the Olympic Games. It is a non-profit-making, tax-deductible organisation, but the government has no interest in it at all; all the money is raised by private subscription. The Chairman is Mr Whitney Stone, without whom the U.S.E.T. would not be in the sound position it is today. An extremely able businessman, he gives tremendous backing to the two trainers employed at Gladstone.

The President of the U.S.E.T. is William Steinkraus – an Olympic gold medallist who, in 1956, had the only two clear rounds in the King George v Gold Cup at the Royal International Horse Show, in London – and is probably one of the three most experienced international show jumpers in the world. Vice-President, Treasurer and Secretary, is George Merck, who has held this important position for some seven or eight years.

The person who has done most to establish Gladstone's riding standards is Bertalan de Nemethy, who is the coach to the United States show jumping team. He was born in 1911 at Gyor in Hungary, and went to the Hungarian Military Academy in Budapest, graduating as a cavalry officer in 1932. He was then called to the Hungarian Cavalry School, receiving the Diploma of Riding Instructor in 1937. He remained at the school, becoming a member of the Hungarian international show jumping team, competing, between 1937 and 1940, in Aachen, Lucerne, Munich, Rome, Florence and Vienna; he was, in fact, in training for the 1940 Olympic Games, which of course were never held. In 1945 he went to Denmark, and after a spell in Switzerland, he emigrated to the United States in 1952, becoming a citizen of that country in 1958. It was in 1955 that he was appointed coach for the U.S.E.T. Amongst the successful riders who have passed through his hands are – in addition to Bill Steinkraus – Frank and Mary Chapot, Hugh Wiley, George Morris, Neal Shapiro, Kathy Kusner, Carol Hofmann, Christine Jones and Robert Ridland.

The other instructor at Gladstone is the former French Olympic rider Jack le Goff, who is responsible for the training of the US international three-day event squad. At present they share the amenities with the international jumping squad; in June 1974 they will move to Hamilton, Massachusetts.

The training programme at Gladstone is of the very highest level. In order to find the best riders to represent the U.S.E.T., screening trials are held regularly, and, in particular, every four years – the year after the Olympic Games. At these trials, which anyone can enter, Bert de Nemethy and one or two others watch very carefully for potential talent.

OPPOSITE *Gladstone: the impressive stable and administrative building* (above); *the ground floor of the stable block where the event horses are stabled* (below).

OVERLEAF *The course at Morven Park is divided into four main areas; riding, stable management, veterinary medicine and instructing.*

Gladstone, New Jersey and Morven Park, Virginia

Any riders thought likely to make international material are asked to consider themselves members of the international squad, and they are expected to attend training sessions at Gladstone. In 1973 the scheme was widened a little: the panel of selectors visited big horse shows around the country, having announced their schedule in advance, with the intention of discovering good riders and horses that had not necessarily voluntarily attended the screening trials. In this way they reckon to bring together some ten or twelve riders, of either sex, to make up the squad for the following season.

In 1973 a total of 103 candidates put themselves forward at the screening trials – anything between twenty and thirty attending each of the trials. From these, eight were chosen to attend Gladstone. Not everyone who is selected for training necessarily remains with the squad for, during the eight weeks – not necessarily consecutive ones – that the riders are assembled at Gladstone, they are further observed by de Nemethy. If a rider is ultimately selected for the squad he is expected to attend when and as requested, and it is likely that if he fails to attend someone else will take his place.

Riders are not necessarily expected to bring their own horses. A feature of Gladstone is the generous loaning of horses, or even donation of horses, by generous and enthusiastic patrons; naturally, if the horses prove unsuitable, they are not accepted and returned. Each rider has two or three horses, though these are interchangeable.

It must be emphasised that the programme at Gladstone has but one aim: the training and maintenance of the US Equestrian Team. As a result, the work at the school is not carried on in classes, but rather in individual training sessions in which a particular rider, or a particular horse, is drilled in some aspect of international competition. These sessions are irregular both in length of time and in frequency; their goal is to bring horse and rider up to the most perfect performance standard of which they are capable.

Much of this training takes place in the main indoor school, or riding hall, called Nautical Hall after the famous show jumper ridden by Hugh Wiley, winner of the King George v Gold Cup in 1959. (Later a successful film was made of this very attractive Palomino horse with the swishing tail.) This school is sixty metres by twenty-six metres, with a small gallery at each end. At one end some jumps are stored, though most of

OPPOSITE *With over three hundred acres of land there is ample room for cross-country riding at Morven Park.* 261

the poles are kept above the kicking boards all round the school, which means that the poles do not have to be carried any great distance. The building is very well lit.

The outdoor sand ring, adjacent to Nautical Hall, is one hundred and thirty metres by fifty-seven; the base is clay with river sand and a top layer of first-grade sand to a total depth of about six inches. It has its own sprinkling system, which works from the side, and the arena is harrowed every day. The only permanent obstacle in this arena is a water jump.

There is another large outdoor schooling ring, only used on special occasions, which has a bank situated in the centre, a Devil's dyke and a water jump. De Nemethy has a strong theory about water jumps, believing that in order to get horses to jump them well, they should be two feet deep on the take-off side, gradually sloping to the landing side which is five inches lower than the take-off side. This, he believes, encourages a horse. The width of the water jump from side to side is seventeen feet.

In another area of the park there are numerous permanent fences – solid stone walls, brush fences, natural rail fences, and the like – for the three-day event horses to school over. Until the three-day event squad moves to Massachusetts, the indoor school will continue to be used alternately by le Goff and de Nemethy with their squads.

The stables are only about fifty yards from Nautical Hall in an old-fashioned, brick building, on two levels, with a loft above the second level; each box is ten feet by ten feet. On the ground level there are twenty-three boxes for the three-day event horses; at the first floor level there are twenty-four boxes where the show jumpers are kept. Communication between the floors is by a gently sloping ramp which is incorporated into the whole building. Each floor has its own feed and tack rooms. The ceilings are of glazed brick and the floors are paved with tiles in herring-bone pattern and central gangways are fourteen feet wide. Some 250 yards away from the stable block is another block of stables where nine horses can be accommodated in boxes eight feet by ten feet. These are used in the summer and are perfectly adequate. Throughout the stables there is an impression of efficiency in every department; the brasswork is highly polished, the tiled floors immaculately clean. Stable management – though the staff is very small – is of a very high order, the staff appearing to be absolutely dedicated.

OPPOSITE *Screening trials at Gladstone; some hopeful candidates.*

Adjoining the main stable block at first floor level, which, due to the sloping ground is on ground level, is the main entrance with the offices on the right and left of the hallway and stables. Above the hall is the trophy room, where all the trophies and rosettes are kept in glass-faced cabinets, the room being carpeted throughout in a very handsome manner and furnished with sofas and comfortable armchairs. This room is used for lectures and also as a room where V.I.P.s can be entertained. It has a large balcony at one end which overlooks the sand arena, so that guests are able to see the horses working out of doors without actually even having to move from the comfort of the lounge.

On the opposite sides of the trophy room are passages leading off to the accommodation for those in training. On one side is the accommodation for male riders, where there are eight separate bedrooms, a living-room, kitchen and bathroom which may be approached from a separate staircase. On the other side there are five separate bedrooms used by grooms, a living-room, kitchen and bathroom, again approached by a separate staircase. There is a large recreation room for table tennis and billiards. Girls are housed in separate accommodation, where there are six bedrooms, a bathroom, living-room and kitchen. It is possible to accommodate up to ten girls by sharing rooms. The permanent stable staff live in cottages on the estate.

Training aids are not normally used at Gladstone – partly because it is felt that video-tape equipment is too expensive, necessitating the employment of an operator; if necessary the equipment is borrowed, but the instructors feel that at this advanced level of instruction video-tape is not really essential. In any case plenty of people use cine cameras and these can always be used for educational purposes if they are thought to be helpful.

There is no doubt that Gladstone is an extremely efficient set-up and also a very happy one; everyone, whether employed or in training, has the greatest affection and respect for both Bert de Nemethy and Jack le Goff. Indeed the United States international teams are most fortunate in the arrangements that are made for them at Gladstone.

If Gladstone trains the exemplars of American riding, the continuation of this tradition of excellence is ensured by the programme of the Morven Park International Equestrian Institute, a school for riding instructors located in the rolling hills of Virginia's Loudoun County,

OPPOSITE *Nautical Hall; a very practical type of cavalletti is used at Gladstone, easy to lift and simple to make (above). The bank, one of the permanent fences in the outdoor jumping arena (below).*

The US three-day event team, trained by Jack le Goff at Gladstone, took the silver medal at the Munich Olympics in 1972.

about an hour's drive from Washington, DC. Morven Park was set up in 1968 to fill the void in top riding instruction left by the phasing out of the American cavalry schools, which had played such an important part in the training of American riders. Its Director, Major John Lynch, would seem to be an important link between the cavalry tradition and the present day: he was an instructor at the British Army

Equitation School at Weedon, as well as at the English military academies of Sandhurst and Woolwich. He has also been coach and trainer to British, Irish and American Olympic Teams, and has competed successfully in dressage, three-day eventing and show jumping; as a result, his approach, and that of the Morven Park instructors' training course, is aimed at producing a well-rounded rider able to perform equally well in the dressage ring, the show jumping arena, and on the steeplechase course.

The curriculum at Morven Park is divided into two segments: the main instructors' course, which lasts nine months from September to June, and a summer session of three four-week courses which can be taken separately or as an eight-week or twelve-week unit. The four-week courses are open to almost anyone with some previous riding experience – but the real business of the school, the nine-month instructors' course, is open only to riders who have reached Pony Club B standard or who have demonstrated a similar equestrian ability. The nine-month course, which can also be applied for credit towards a Bachelor of Science degree at Springfield College, Springfield, Massachusetts, is divided into two sections, the better to put into practice Major Lynch's description of the school's programme – 'to teach people to teach after they've been taught themselves'. The first half of the instructors' course is devoted to the latter part of this proposition, with students receiving intensive instruction in riding and schooling; the second half of the course puts the emphasis on teaching. Students also receive a thorough grounding in stable management, veterinary medicine, and elementary farriery, both in theoretical form – through lectures – and in practice. All feeding, grooming, mucking out, and maintenance of tack is done by the students, a facet of the curriculum that shows how necessity can be the mother of invention. In the first year of the school's existence considerable operating deficits made it imperative that the school's staff be drastically cut back, and so the students were put to work in the stables instead of merely in the lecture halls, to their own and the school's mutual benefit.

The instructors' course, like the four-week summer courses, is mainly made up of boarding students, who live either in the school's three dormitories – one-storey white cottages with several bedrooms, baths and a sitting-room – or in rented quarters in the nearby town of Lees-

Some of America's successful international riders: Bill Steinkraus on Snowbound winning the individual gold medal at the Mexico Olympics (top); Kathy Kusner on Nirvana schooling in Nautical Hall (above); Michael Owen Page and Grasshopper at the Rome Olympics (top right); George Morris on High Noon at the Royal International Horse Show, London, 1960 (bottom right).
OVERLEAF *A student display in front of the Morven Park mansion.*

burg. They take all meals in the cafeteria, a low, pleasant building with windows overlooking the barns on one side and the two outdoor *manèges* on the other. Lectures are held either in the main lecture hall or on the spot in the stables or the indoor riding school. The stables are at present made up of three main stable blocks, airy, well-lit buildings with rows of looseboxes and two or three small but impeccably kept tack rooms. The horses – there are eighty of them – are all Thoroughbreds, some lent to the school, others donated as gifts, and some purchased. Many of them have been champions in their various fields, and many will go on to successful competition outside the school; others are still quite green and have only begun to show what they can do. Outside one of the barns is a well-worn circle of dust surrounding a hummock of turf where the horses are exercised on the lunge rein; beyond that are paddocks for grazing, and beyond these an excellent new cross-country course.

At the beginning of the instructors' course the students are arbitrarily divided into two or three groups or 'rides', and every day each group

OPPOSITE *Major John Lynch, the Director of Morven Park, on The Regent, an experienced three-day event horse; the school has several former Olympic horses, invaluable in showing students how well a horse can go.*
ABOVE *Sir Winston Churchill presents The Prince of Wales Cup to Major Lynch on Irish Boy, 1949.*

The school's three dormitories can house twenty-four students.

The emblem of the school on the cover of the prospectus.

Out on the cross-country course; the school buildings in the background.

works out for two periods in the indoor school or, weather permitting, in the outdoor *manèges* under the supervision of the group's instructor – there are two or three assistant instructors working under the direction of Major Lynch.

At the same time other 'rides' are having lectures on such subjects as showing jumpers, the importance of feed supplements, principles of dressage, the uses of the cavalletti, and the like. There are also demonstrations of various aspects of the art of riding at which all the riders attend together. Twice a week the school veterinarian gives lectures or practical demonstrations. Once the students have been drilled to ride well enough so that they can also demonstrate correctly, they are trained to teach, and a highlight of this part of the course is a week in which each student takes on the supervision of his fellows. At the beginning of the week, the student files a complete plan with his instructor: it includes a daily schedule, an outline of lectures and demonstrations, a complete feed schedule for each horse, a shoeing roster and grooming list for each horse, and designs for any courses to be ridden over in classes or demonstrations. The student 'instructor' is responsible for the well-being of students and horses alike during his

OPPOSITE AND ABOVE *Working in the indoor school; once students have been taught to sit correctly and have developed a fairly active seat, they are taught dressage up to Olympic three-day event standard.*

week of command – a unique preparation for the day when that responsibility will be his job.

At the end of the nine-month course all students must have satisfied their instructors that they have learnt all that the school has tried to teach them in the four areas of training. Major Lynch and the instructors judge their pupils' performance in riding technique, instruction, and stable management, and the veterinarian judges their skill in veterinary medicine. Only then – in an exuberant graduation ceremony in which both horses and riders take part – are the students awarded the Morven Park Instructors' Certificate – grade A, B, or C. The Certificate is testimony to their months of hard work, and to their thorough background in all equestrian matters, from the loosebox to the lecture hall to the riding ring.

Whereas Gladstone concentrates entirely on the international squads, Morven is devoted to the training of top-class instructors: it is hoped that the influence of Morven will eventually be as great as the influence of Gladstone. There can be little doubt that the existence of Gladstone

ABOVE AND OPPOSITE *The students are divided into two or three rides under the supervision of a full-time instructor. Each instructor is responsible for approximately fifteen students.*

has played a very considerable part in improving horse show standards and has also increased enormously the number of people in America who now ride in the educated and classical style typified by the riders who have been trained by de Nemethy. The prominence of these riders has also aroused a much greater general interest in riding amongst ordinary people. All through America riding centres have sprung up to cater to this new interest in the Olympic disciplines. One of the most popular and productive of these, the Potomac Horse Centre in Gaithersburg, Maryland, gives a twelve-week horsemasters' course, which is

PREVIOUS PAGES *Schooling on long reins: the rein back (top left); the half pass to the right (bottom left); changing tracks at the canter (top right); the half pass to the left (bottom right).*

invariably over-subscribed. A fellow of the British Horse Society, Miss Betty Howett, is Director and Chief Instructor, and Gaithersburg is the only school in the USA that is authorised by the British Horse Society to hold B.H.S.A.I. and B.H.S.I. examinations.

Gaithersburg, which, like Morven Park, is close to Washington, also allows its amenities to be used by occasional and recreational riders. These amenities are considerable, including as they do two full-sized indoor arenas, ample stabling and an outdoor *manège*, together with

OPPOSITE *A young horse jumping on the lunge rein. The side poles are placed so that the trainer has no need to raise his hand, and risk interfering with the horse's head, during the jump.* ABOVE *With long reins the trainer is able to judge pace and distance accurately and horses apt to rush their fences can be taught to jump calmly.* OVERLEAF *Students and members of the Loudoun Hunt returning home after a day's hunting.*

ABOVE AND OPPOSITE *In the stables at Morven Park. Students are expected to learn all aspects of stable management by practical application.*

sufficient land on which to hold a one-day event, with a two-mile cross-country course. There is also a horse-breeding farm.

Perhaps a national centre or school of riding is not even necessary in the United States. Certainly, with the classical example set by the riders from Gladstone, and the perpetuation of high instructional standards

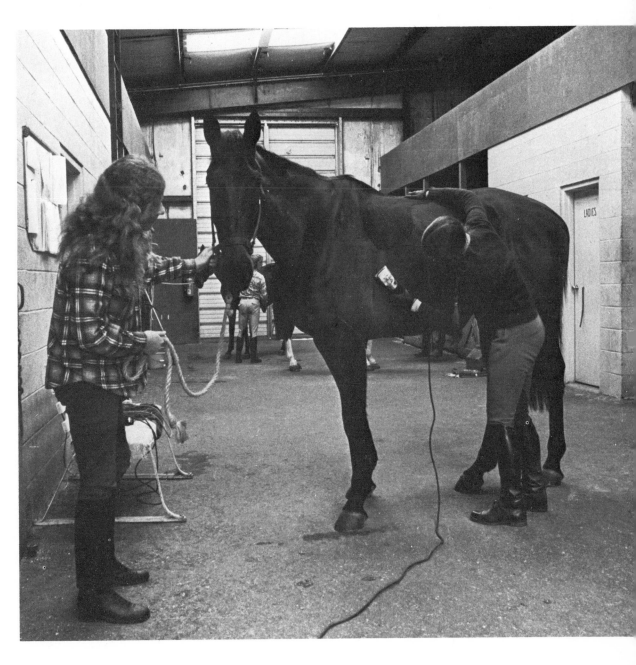

A demonstration of precision as the riders take the bank simultaneously in opposite directions. The grey horse then jumps across the fence and out over the pole.

that is now being achieved at Morven Park, the state of the art is very healthy indeed. And with the example of brilliant international riding continually supported by the training of first-rate instructors, such regional centres as the one at Gaithersburg should continue to thrive, ensuring a tradition of informed and dedicated horsemanship in America.

OPPOSITE *Immaculately turned out, one of the students, George Parfitt, competes in the 1970 Blue Ridge Event, on Jomo (above); watched by Major Lynch, a student takes the San Sebastian in fine style (below).*
ABOVE *An exercise to develop an independent seat; the student, without reins or stirrups, removes his coat down a line of fences.*

TOP *At the end of the nine-month course successful students are awarded the Morven Park Instructors'
Certificate ; the 1973 graduation class.* ABOVE *The Regent, ridden by Jimmy Wofford, winning the National
Championship in 1971.* OPPOSITE *Two of the instructors from Morven Park.*

Eire

Burton Hall, Herbertstown

PREVIOUS PAGES *An old log provides a perfect practice fence for students at Burton Hall.*
OPPOSITE *In promoting advanced training and practical horsemanship, Burton Hall has been very much the spearhead of equitation in Ireland.*

Eire

Few would dispute the belief that Ireland produces some of the best horses in the world. This is due to a number of reasons. To begin with, there has long been a great tradition of horse-breeding in Ireland, although this is, unfortunately, not quite so much the case today; but until recently even quite small farmers all over Ireland kept a few mares and, thanks to their experience, carefully chose suitable stallions with the result that there seemed to be an almost limitless supply of good young horses. Hence the famous fairs held all over the country where, until a few years ago, useful horses could be bought comparatively cheaply – though within years, or even months, they were often worth at least ten times the original price. Moreover, Ireland has the added advantage in that it experiences a mild balmy climate conducive to successful breeding. It is possible, and practical, to leave mares and foals out all year round to benefit from the lush grass. In the breeding areas it is the rich limestone soil that ensures exactly the sort of nourishment that lays the foundation for the splendid bone structure associated with the Irish horses: horses for which there is always a ready international market. It is worth mentioning just a handful of Irish-bred horses that have contributed to this country's extraordinary reputation: My Swallow and Vaguely Noble, on the flat; Arkle, Bula and Red Rum in National Hunt racing; Ambassador, Stroller and Pennwood Forge Mill in show jumping; High and Mighty, Lochinvar and Durlas Eile in three-day eventing; Little Model in dressage.

A strong element of commercialism has sustained the horse in Ireland. Indeed it has been said that Ireland is one great sale yard. Certainly the *raison d'être* of the famed Dublin Horse Show at Ballsbridge is the selling of Irish-bred horses. The international jumping is so often just titillation for a great horse occasion when the real function of the show is to provide an arena for the horses to display their potential, both under saddle and in hand. For a long time it has been considered the best place to find potential champions, and winners will fetch very high prices at subsequent sales. As a result of this emphasis on breeding and selling, it is, perhaps, inevitable that there has been less concentration on educated riding or instruction.

Paradoxically, it was the brilliant instruction of the foreign-trained Colonel Paul Rodzianko that first drew the attention of the world to Ireland as a centre of horsemanship. The trainer for the Irish army jumping team between the wars, Paul Rodzianko had not only been a pupil of the legendary Caprilli (another of whose students was the father of Piero and Raimondo d'Inzeo) but he also studied under James Fillis, one of the greatest names in equitation and for long, though an Englishman, riding master at the Imperial School in Russia, as well as the author of the classic *Breaking and Riding*. Rodzianko did his masters credit and it was he who was responsible in the thirties for producing such riders as Jed O'Dwyer, Dan Corry and Jack Lewis, and the horses Limerick Lace, Red Hugh and Tramore Bay. Another rider whom he trained, though not for the Irish team as he was at the time an officer in the Scots Greys, was Joe Dudgeon who among many other international triumphs won the King George v Gold Cup at Olympia. Probably his best horse was Goblet.

Shortly before the war Colonel Joe Hume Dudgeon started his famous riding establishment at Merville just outside Dublin. He had recently retired from the army, where he had served as equitation officer at the Royal Military College, Sandhurst. He brought with him to Ireland Sergeant-Major Fraser McMaster who was associated with the school until his death in 1968. The school's traditions were, therefore, those of the British cavalry. Again we can see the great debt that civilian riding owes to cavalry training.

During the Second World War Joe Dudgeon's daughter Kathleen, now Mrs de Vere Hunt, a Fellow of the British Horse Society and herself a successful show jumper, helped her mother run the school until Colonel Dudgeon was demobilised. In 1953 the school moved to larger premises, Burton Hall, a charming property close to Dublin and a few miles from Merville. The emphasis at the school continued to be very much on practical riding, as is obvious when one realises that such horses as Sea Spray, Go Lightly, Grasshopper, Loughlin, Fru and Foster, all came from Burton Hall and made their names in the early days after the move. The successes of the school justified considerable expansion, for not only could Burton Hall be regarded as the most successful school in Ireland, but also as one of the best in the world.

The reputation of Burton Hall has rested largely on the superb staff that it has attracted. Of great assistance to Colonel Dudgeon in the fifties and early sixties was Penny Moreton, a brilliant and attractive horsewoman with a uniquely sensitive touch, who not only achieved

Ireland's reputation as a producer of top class horses is undisputed; a reputation that rests in part on the extraordinary success of Irish-bred horses in all major equestrian sports. On the racecourse, great horses like Arkle and Vaguely Noble, in the show jumping arena, Stroller, Marian Mould's little horse, who won a silver medal at the Mexico Olympics (left), and Pennwood Forge Mill, ridden by Paddy McMahon to win the Men's European Championship and the King George V Gold Cup in 1973 (below); and in eventing, High and Mighty, with Sheila Wilcox, winner of the Badminton Horse Trials in successive years, 1957 and 1958 (opposite).

Eire

ABOVE AND OPPOSITE *The reputation of Burton Hall has rested largely on the superb staff it has attracted.*
Sylvia Stanier, a most talented horsewoman, specialises in training young horses and in dressage but here gives
classes on more general aspects of horsemanship, shoeing and the care of the horse.

fame by representing Ireland in the three-day event team in 1966 when Ireland won the World Championship, and later in the Olympic team, but also gave great pleasure in a charming display at the Horse of the Year Show in 1962 when she rode her horse Korbous without a bridle.

Her place was subsequently taken by Sylvia Stanier, whose mother Lady Stanier was a distinguished judge at the Dublin Horse Show for many years, and whose teachers included not only Colonel Joe Dudgeon but also the great Swedish Olympic medallist Schmidt-Jensen, and Nuño Oliviera, the Portuguese master whose finesse, lightness and beauty of riding has so influenced modern dressage thinking. A most talented person with a horse, Sylvia Stanier gave an effective display at the Horse of the Year Show in 1966 with Le Marquis, driven on long reins. In addition she has ridden the Dublin champions Lough Thorn and Bachelor Gay, but at Burton Hall she specialises in the training of young horses and dressage.

Not surprisingly both the successes of horses and riders from Burton Hall and the prowess of the resident instructors have spread the school's fame far and wide. One of the results of this international renown is its strong ties with the United States, many American pupils travelling across the Atlantic specially for instruction and training at Burton Hall.

The aims of the school are to give a really thorough basic grounding in equitation on the lines originally laid down by Colonel Dudgeon.

303

Eire

Pupils are prepared for the British Horse Society's examinations, and the school is more than adequately adapted to these demands. As the school keeps a number of horses capable of jumping a fair-sized course of show jumps, as well as many horses trained to a high level in dressage, pupils at Burton Hall are invariably taught on well-trained animals. This is a vital aspect of teaching. A rider can learn more advanced equitation only on a properly trained horse.

Ian Dudgeon on Go Lightly at the White City, London, in 1952.

Jumping instruction at Burton Hall has traditionally been of an exceptionally high standard as not only was the founder Colonel Dudgeon one of the most successful show jumpers between the wars, and indeed in the early post-war years, but his son Ian, who took over from his father in 1968, has achieved considerable fame. He represented Ireland in the three-day event in the Olympic Games in 1952, 1956 and 1960. In show jumping he twice won the Daily Telegraph Cup and once the Country Life and Riding Cup at the Horse of the Year Show on Go Lightly. On five occasions he has won the National Championship at the Royal Dublin Society Show at Ballsbridge. Twice he has won the International Championship, on one occasion winning both the National Championship and the International Championship on the same day.

In 1973 the school had to make a second move when Dublin County Council compulsorily purchased their property. That a school can so successfully survive two big moves in twenty years speaks well of its resilience and, of course, its reputation. Captain Dudgeon was fortunate in finding a property some twenty miles outside Dublin in Herbertstown, County Meath, near the famous Fairyhouse racecourse. Amenities here are excellent with a large indoor school (sixty by twenty-five metres) and a more than adequate outdoor arena, a jumping paddock and a cross-country course. There are more than twenty loose-boxes in the excellent stable yard. In addition to the horses stabled in the main yard, there are twenty horses and ponies accommodated for pupils. Horses can also be taken at livery for schooling.

Burton Hall has been very much the spearhead of equitation in Ireland. As might be expected in that country, there has for long been an almost insouciant approach to educational riding, indeed to anything organised in the horse world. This is now changing. In 1971 the Irish Horse Board came into being with valuable and comprehensive terms of reference. Its purpose is to promote and develop the Irish horse industry as follows:

BREEDING DEVELOPMENT

To aid marketing of Irish horses a breeding committee, formed by the board and including representatives of several interested organisations, is now at work on formulating a general breeding policy and on setting up a non-Thoroughbred register. This long-awaited register will be of great importance to buyers and breeders alike. It will make possible the issue of pedigree certificates, furnish background information and keep records of the performances of those horses entered on it. In the meantime various schemes to encourage breeders and to improve breeding standards have been introduced.

SALES DIRECTORY

For overseas buyers the Horse Board maintains a sales directory which provides information on the sources of supply and the prices of all varieties of Irish horses and ponies. The Board will help to arrange introductions to Irish breeders, owners and exporters and in general will assist the potential buyer in every possible way.

FARRIERY

With a view to reviving and developing the craft of farriery, the Irish Horse Board initiated a Farriery Apprenticeship Scheme in 1971. Under the terms of this scheme suitable young men are awarded bursaries to serve an apprenticeship of three years with well-qualified master farriers throughout the country. The training programme is such that the best practical features of the indigenous craft are combined with relevant aspects of veterinary science to give a modern technological dimension to what was up to recently a dying art.

NATIONAL EQUESTRIAN CENTRE

Plans are being prepared for the establishment of an extensive National Equestrian Centre by the Irish Horse Board. This centre will provide training facilities to benefit all equitation interests in the country. One of the Board's chief aims is to enable horses and riders to receive top class instruction and thereby assist in the formation of future Irish international show jumping teams.

When one recognises that in five years the value of horses exported from Ireland rose from £6,400,000 ($15 million) in 1969 to nearly £12 million ($30 million) in 1973, one can then appreciate the need of such an organisation and the immense contribution that it can make to everything to do with the horse in Ireland. The proposal for a national centre can only be beneficial.

OPPOSITE Students get practical experience in all aspects of horsemanship – not least mucking out (above). Foxhunting is a traditional and popular sport in Ireland and the Irish hunter, clever and surefooted, is in growing demand from overseas buyers (below).

Eire

ABOVE *Some of the students at Burton Hall. The school attracts students from many parts of the world but especially from the United States.* OPPOSITE *Ian Dudgeon took over at Burton Hall in 1968 and has carried on the pioneering work of his father, Colonel Joe Dudgeon.*

As far as riding and in particular advanced equitation is concerned, Ireland owes much to Burton Hall, to Ian Dudgeon and to his father whose pioneering efforts he has advanced; and, of course to Iris Kellett who, when she eventually retired from the show ring, started her own extremely successful school at Ballsbridge. Twice winner of the Queen Elizabeth II Gold Cup at the Royal International Horse Show in London, on Rusty in 1949, its inaugural year, and again two years later, she won the Ladies European Championship no less than twenty years later on Morning Light (now owned by the French and called Moet et Chandon). She quickly achieved success as a riding school proprietress when in 1970 she produced young Eddie Macken on her two good horses, Oatfield Hills and Easter Parade. It is, perhaps, the singular feature of the riding schools in Ireland that they are actively involved in producing top-class horses from their schools: Go Lightly and Easter Parade are both examples. But this would seem to be entirely in keeping with the character of the Irish. Essentially they are active, rather than passive people. This is why Ireland has produced so many brilliant horsemen and horsewomen in all aspects of riding. It is wholly admirable that Ireland should now be following a lead given more than thirty years ago by Colonel Joe Dudgeon in developing this more serious side of horsemanship.

The first chapter in this book told of the famous Spanish Riding School of Vienna. Burton Hall could not be more different; yet in many ways it is Burton Hall that underlines the development and the increasing importance of the riding school movement the world over. The Spanish Riding School is the ultimate in a specialist aspect of equestri-

309

anism: *haute école*. Obviously there is a place for it and it has a vital role to play. Vienna, however, is for the few – while it is the many today who want riding instruction, and in a simple, unsophisticated way Captain Ian Dudgeon is developing Burton Hall along the lines that increasingly fulfil these needs. In a completely unostentatious manner the threads of so many of the greatest traditions of the past are woven together: Ireland is singularly well suited to follow the principles of Caprilli, handed down through Rodzianko and Colonel Joe Dudgeon, which can be summed up as follows: as far as possible a horse should be allowed to jump in the free style that is its natural way. It should be permitted as much initiative as possible. (By contrast, for instance, the emphasis in Germany is on discipline – control of the horse.)

It is the all-round horseman that Burton Hall, reflecting the trend of the modern school, is trying to produce. In Ireland today, as all over the world, the vital importance of proper basic training has now been appreciated. A good show jumper is a better show jumper if it has had a sound training on the ground – dressage. A good cross-country horse is a better cross-country horse if it is properly balanced; balance being acquired only through correct basic training. The same goes for the rider. Ireland is particularly fortunate in that its horses have learned to look after themselves over the Irish hunting countries. They are clever and balanced. Many riders may be 'naturals', but training is needed if the natural is to become 'professional'.

It is the many contrasting methods and principles that are so fascinating. Yet all the schools, apparently so different, are striving towards the same ends: to improve the standard of equitation and to improve the standard of instruction. The traditional schools such as Vienna and Saumur have been a great influence since the Second World War. National schools, with state assistance, have played a vital part. The independent schools also have a part to play; because of their independence they have the ability to experiment and expand as they will.

With the explosion of interest in riding the world over, the great riding schools, in every country where they exist, have a common responsibility. They may have the glamour and status of the legendary Vienna; they may have the simple unsophistication of Burton Hall; each has a greater or lesser influence on world equitation, but an influence nevertheless.

Ian Dudgeon instructing. An important aspect of the instruction at Burton Hall is that pupils are invariably taught on well-trained horses, in the belief – a belief also emphasised in Vienna – that a rider can learn more advanced equitation only on a properly trained horse.

Glossary

Aids The signals conveyed to the horse by movement of the legs, contact with the horse's mouth through the reins, and the voice.

Balance A well-balanced horse is one carrying its own weight and that of its rider so that it can easily use and control itself.

Ballotade see *croupade*.

Barrage A 'jump-off' in show jumping.

Behind the bit When the horse appears to avoid the bit or is frightened of it.

Capriole A horse is trained for the *capriole* as he is for the *croupade* except that in the *capriole* the horse is tapped with the whip on the point of the shoulder and then immediately on the haunches so that he raises all four legs, the hind legs kicking out to the rear.

Cavalletti From the Italian, *cavalletti* means literally 'little horse' and refers to poles, usually set on cross-pieces, used in the training of horses.

Cavesson A head-piece with a heavy nose-band and three rings used for lungeing.

Chef d'équipe Captain or manager of an equestrian team.

Collection The foundation stone of all dressage since from it springs the lightness of action that is the goal and purpose of dressage. It consists of making the horse dispose the various parts of his body in the manner best suited to the distribution of his own weight, thereby rendering every movement more flowing and functional.

Combination A fence comprising two or more separate elements at a distance not more than 39′ 4″ from each other. The usual combination fences are doubles or trebles.

Contact The link through the reins between a rider's hands and the horse's mouth.

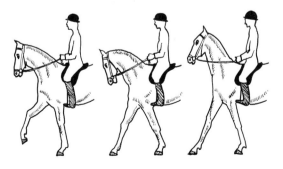

LEFT *correct contact* CENTRE *behind the bit* RIGHT *above the bit*

Glossary

Courbette The *courbette* is an air that evolved from the *levade*. In this air the horse raises himself from the ground with the forelegs well drawn in, and then jumps and lands on his hind legs without touching the ground with his forefeet.

Croupade For the *croupade* the horse raises his forelegs slightly and then brings them down and immediately raises his hind legs, and draws them under. Such an air is of necessity taught between pillars. The horse is secured by a halter and shanks and then is collected. When he responds well, the trainer taps him with the whip on the right shoulder, and as soon as the horse has risen he taps him behind the girth. The forelegs come down and the hind legs are thrust upward. A *croupade* in which the horse draws in his hind legs so that the shoes are visible from behind is called a *ballotade*, and is the first stage of the *capriole*.

Disunited When a horse uses his legs in the wrong sequence.

Dressage The training to give the horse the utmost harmoniousness of movement and to allow the animal to demonstrate his perfect susceptibility and obedience to the will of the rider.

Ecuyer The French word for equerry, squire or horseman, *écuyer* is also the name given to the riders, traditionally commissioned officers, who make up part of the *Cadre Noir* at Saumur.

Forward Seat The method of sitting a horse now commonly used in equestrian sports, and generally attributed to Federico Caprilli.

Hackamore A bitless bridle.

Half-pass When a horse goes diagonally forward and sideways on two tracks.

Haute Ecole This is a development of simple dressage (the exaltation and consequence of dressage). In its airs above the ground *haute école* is schooling for virtuoso performance. While it is true that a spirited horse in the wild will execute certain acrobatics, with a man in the saddle these movements must be done on command and in accordance with certain definite rules of style. *Haute école* distinguishes between low, intermediate and high airs. To the first category belong those airs in which the horse does not leave the ground; the second category includes the *pesade* and *courbette*; and the third the *capriole, ballotade* and *levade*.

High School see *haute école*.

Impulsion Forward movement motivated by the strong use of the hocks.

Levade Rather like the *pesade*, although the height of the body from the ground is reduced, the body being held at an angle of thirty degrees. The horse is elevated with his forelegs tucked in without moving forward, keeping his hind legs in place. In the air, the horse must bend and rest on his haunches, keeping his head in place and almost touch his elbows with his hooves.

Long-reining Driving of a young horse by the trainer on foot, before he is backed, thus getting used to a bit in his mouth without being worried by the weight of a rider on his back.

Lungeing Correct lungeing is an art, and does not mean just making the horse run around in a circle. The main object of lungeing is to gain the horse's confidence, make him obedient to the rider's will and teach him to balance himself without a rider; it is also helpful for exercising the horse and training riders.

Work on the lunge

Manège A confined area in which a horse can be given concentrated schooling.

Militaire A continental name for the three-day event, also known as *concours complet*.

Near-side The left-hand side of a horse.

Off-side The right-hand side of a horse.

On the bit When a horse is on a steady, firm contact with the bit.

Over-bent When the head is carried in close to the neck in an exaggerated arched position.

Glossary

Oxer A brush fence with a pole on the take-off side; a double-oxer usually has a pole on each side.

Passage A high school air consisting of a cadenced, hesitating trot.

Passage

Pesade The *pesade* is performed by raising the forelegs off the ground and drawing them in while balancing the body on bent hind legs, the body forming an angle of forty-five degrees to the ground. The horse, collected and advancing at a slow gait, is signalled by the reins and strong leg pressure, thus causing him to lean on his haunches and thrust upward and forward with his forehands, as if he were jumping an obstacle but keeping his legs planted on the ground.

Piaffe This is the collected trot in place. The horse's back is supple and the hindquarters, with active hocks, are well engaged giving great freedom and lightness to the action of the forelegs.

Piaffe

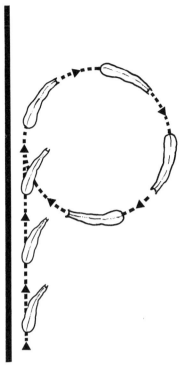

Transition from shoulder-in into a volte

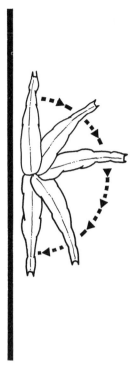

Turn on the haunches

Pirouette This is the turn on the haunches in four to five strides to a collected canter. The horse, with hocks well engaged, does the turn with its hind legs completing the smallest circle, almost on the spot, with the forelegs describing a wider circle around the hind legs.

Prix des Nations A team event in show jumping.

Puissance A 'test' competition with a few, but very big fences.

Quadrille Performed particularly by the riders of the Spanish Riding School, it is the traditional conclusion of the performance. Four, eight or twelve riders demonstrate the finesse and co-ordinated movement achieved through careful training.

Shoulder-in A movement on two tracks, the quarters following a straight line while the shoulders, head and neck are bent inwards: a training exercise.

Spread Fence A fence which incorporates width as well as height.

Triple Bar A fence of the 'staircase' variety, with three poles on separate supports, each higher than the one in front. Frequently interspersed with bushes, this is the easiest of types of obstacle to jump.

Two-track A movement in which the hind legs follow a separate track to the forelegs.

Upright A fence in one vertical plane, usually poles or planks, which requires only an upward effort from the horse.

Index

Acknowledgments for Photographs

The author and publishers would like to thank John Hedgecoe who photographed most of the illustrations in this book and the following who kindly supplied additional material:

ARCHÃOLOGISCHES MUSEUM, ISTANBUL 14–15;
ASSOCIATED PRESS 268 (*above*), 269 (*above and below*), 300 (*below*);
FOTOGRAF OSCAR EILERT 104 (*below*), *107*, *108* (*above and below*), 112 (*above*);
HIRMER FOTOARCHIV 14–15;
KEYSTONE PRESS AGENCY 165, 168, 171, 246, 247, 300 (*above*), 301, 304;
MARY EVANS PICTURE LIBRARY 19 (*below*), 20 (*above*), 26 (*below*);
MONTY 206, 210, 211, 213, 217, 218;
MORVEN PARK INTERNATIONAL EQUESTRIAN INSTITUTE 250, *258–9*, *260*, 270–1, 272, 273, 274, 275, 276 (*above and below*), 277, 278, 279 (*above and below*), 280 (*above and below*), 281 (*above and below*), 282, 283, 284–5, 286, 287, 288–9, 290 (*above and below*), 291, 292 (*above and below*), *293*;
NOVOSTI PRESS AGENCY 116 (*below*), 120, 121 (*below*), 122, 126 (*above and below*), 127, 128 (*above and below*), 130 (*above and below*), 132 (*above and below*), 134 (*left and below*), 135 (*right and far right*);
PRISCILLA E. PHIPPS 116 (*left*), 121 (*above*), 124;
R. REAL 140 (*above, centre and below*);
ROGER VIOLLET 18, 19 (*right*), 20 (*left*), 22, 26 (*above*), 28 (*left and right*);
SPANISCHE REITSCHULE, VIENNA 30–1, 34–5, 36, 37, 38, 39, *41*, *44*, 47 (*right and far right*), 50;
VOTAVA, *42–3*, 48;
ELSIE E. WISE 253 (*above and below*), 254–5, *257* (*above and below*), 263 (*above and below*), 264 (*above and below*), 266, 268 (*below*).

Numbers in italic indicate colour illustrations.